With *The Depolarizing of America*, Kirk Schneider has created a remarkable process for helping to rebuild our democracy one relationship at a time, from the level of ordinary citizens to that of public leaders. The "Experiential Democracy Dialogue" is a gift to a nation that badly needs healing.

William J. Doherty, PhD, is a professor of Family Social Science at the University of Minnesota and co-founder of Braver Angels

Once again, Kirk Schneider has challenged us to claim our humanity or ignite our own self-imposed psychological and physical demise. It is extremely important to note that in the face of the worldwide coronavirus pandemic, much of the United States has become more explicitly polarized. *The Depolarizing of America: A Guidebook for Social Healing* provides relevant historical contexts that spawned much of the divisiveness of today, as well as a blueprint for optimal engagement in bridging those differences. I applaud Schneider's clarity in centering the "fear" that divides us. I am reminded of the insightful quote from the character, "Fear," from Pixar's moving 2015 film, Inside/Outside. *"Alright, we did not die today! I'd call that an unqualified success."* However, should we not expect more in determining the "success" of humanity? Should we be so bold as to determine that the success of humanity is not just living yet *how* we live? Schneider's timely work contributes to our capacity to raise up other emotions and ways of being that are necessary to balance "fear" in promoting civility and collective sanity. I, for one, am counting on the complex-simplicity of the experiential democracy dialogues that Schneider is inviting us to engage in for the sake of humanity; to do otherwise is a frightening thought!

Theopia Jackson, PhD, Chair, Clinical Psychology Program, Saybrook University; President, Association of Black Psychologists

This book offers a much-needed bridge to heal the many divides we see in the world today through a novel awe-based approach. Kirk Schneider is one of my favorite existential-humanistic psychologists, and when he offers spiritual and humanitarian guidance, I listen.

Scott Barry Kaufman, PhD, author of *Transcend: The New Science of Self-Actualization*, host of *The Psychology Podcast*

D1474635

In *The Depolarizing of America: A Guidebook for Social Healing,* Schneider presents a brilliant analysis of dogmatic mindsets that bring noxious effects to the world. In delineating the psychological components that operate beneath polarized minds, Schneider highlights the role and function of awe in developing wakefulness, mindfulness and togetherness in recuperating from social malaise. Schneider's work is promising, illuminating, and thought provoking. His exegesis is of existential significance as it presents a remarkable exploration of our global entrapment and addresses our ontological angst in a world surrounded by sundry manifestations of unrest, tension, turmoil, and bitterness.

Sayyed Mohsen Fatemi, PhD, Adjunct Faculty, York University, Canada;
Author of *The Psychology of Inner Peace (Heartfulness),*
Cambridge University Press

Drawing on his life's work in healing divisions in the soul through awe-based therapy, Kirk Schneider offers crisp, practical guidelines for anyone who wants to use awe-based dialogue to bind the divisions polarizing our families, communities, and politics. This gem of a book will help us learn how to heal our social wounds and revitalize our collective soul.

Robert Kramer, PhD, author of *The Birth of Relationship Therapy: Carl Rogers Meets Otto Rank,* organizational consultant, visiting professor of social psychology at Corvinus University of Budapest

I've had the pleasure of participating in a handful of Experiential Democracy workshops, including one shared in this book, and they have been, without doubt, some of the more transformative experiences I have had. In this time of extreme polarization, it is easy to hunker down on our "sides" but much harder to reach across the divide. Experiential democracy and the ideas presented in this timely work are the tools we can use to begin to heal the divide in our world. When we are able to hold both our humanity and others, our ability to sit with complicated differences becomes that much easier. When we stop seeing the other as "other" but rather as a human being, we can hold space with kindness and dignity, even if we fundamentally disagree. This book is a timely read for anyone who wants to have, or facilitate, difficult conversations around the issues of our time.

Lisa Vallejos, PhD, Chair, Rocky Mountain Humanistic Counseling and Psychological Association; co-founder, The Humanitarian Alliance

Kirk Schneider succinctly describes healthy communication processes that effectively diffuse polarizing differences while inspiring intellectual curiosity, empathy, compassion, and hope for a better tomorrow. Through structured, safe, and mindful communication formats, readers will discover how participants can unpack differences, focus on commonalities, and relinquish fear and anger associated with personal and group stereotypes, identity politics, myths, and other important issues. This book lays out a cogent vision of virtuous dialogue possibilities that could be broadly used within divisive political processes, schools, religious settings, and other institutions, as well as a means to bridge the divides with historically marginalized communities. The author provides relevant examples, including one involving a police officer that provides a future framework for law enforcement agencies to participate with their most vocal critics. *The Depolarizing of America* plants the seeds to break down many of the differences separating people today.

Jason Jones, a police professional
and criminal justice educator based in Portland, Oregon

When we know that alienation, fueled by polarization, breeds suffering, and authentic engagement via dialogue is our only hope for healing such alienation, though we are unsure how to proceed, Kirk Schneider's work on polarization is indeed a genuine balm. Schneider calls us out of the privacy of the therapeutic consulting room and into global theaters where we must link arms and march together into challenges of pandemic viruses, sustainability, global warming, extreme and persistent poverty and violence, trafficking, starvation, the degradation of animal and plant kin, just to clear our throats. But we will quickly halt in our tracks with any and all of these challenges unless we see and address polarization. This book, therefore, is necessary for our survival, and is, finally, a concrete pathway into democracy with so much more substance than the typical, vapid clucking so often offered by political rhetoric. Bravo!

Todd DuBose, PhD, Faculty, Chicago School of Professional Psychology

Kirk Schneider's "Guidebook for Social Healing" provides a valuable tool in our quest to depolarize America, starting with ourselves. As someone who practices what he preaches by leading depolarization workshops, Dr. Schneider is able to insightfully share with readers his awe-inspired approach to depolarization. During Braver Angels events, I have witnessed the way Dr. Schneider brings people together in the spirit of curiosity, and—as a member of Braver Angels—I hope to emulate his approach. His book is a great resource for doing that!

Ruth Littmann Ashkenazi, Member of Braver Angels

As I write this emphatic endorsement of Dr. Schneider's new work, a world-wide pandemic is raging all around us. The rapidly changing conditions experienced due to this viral outbreak have fueled the fires of epidemics long simmering underneath this plague in America: the epidemics of poverty, health disparities, inequity, racism, and profound othering. How does one hope in such uncertainty and violence? We hope wisely and to do so calls one to engage radical imagination, an embrace of the unknown and a skilled mentor. Kirk Schneider has been a powerful mentor to many. This new book, *The Depolarizing of America*, offers a brilliant invitation to Wise Hope and Social Healing in our troubled times.

Gina Subia Belton, PhD, Psychology professor at Saybrook University, Thanatologist, Existential Medicine

To Nitza + Ofer,
Comrades in the quest –
Contributors to the cause.
With much
admiration,
Kirk
17 Nov.
2020

The Depolarizing of America:
A Guidebook for Social Healing

By Kirk J. Schneider

University
PROFESSORS PRESS

Colorado Springs, CO
www.universityprofessorspress.com

First Published in 2020, University Professors Press.

Print ISBN: 978-1-939686-63-3
ebook ISBN: 978-1-939686-64-0

University Professors Press
Colorado Springs, CO
www.universityprofessorspress.com

Cover Design by Laura Ross
Cover screenshot by David DeGroot and courtesy of Society of Humanistic Psychology, adapted by Louis Hoffman
Back Cover Photo by Jurate Raulinaitis

Dedication

To Martin Buber and *The Life of Dialogue*; and to James Baldwin who penned: "Not everything that is faced can be changed, but nothing can be changed until it is faced."

Table of Contents

Preface

Disarmament, with mutual honor and confidence, is a continuing imperative. Together we must learn how to compose differences, not with arms, but with intellect and decent purpose.

> ~ Dwight D. Eisenhower's "Military–Industrial Complex" Speech, 1961

I don't want to be the president who builds empires...I want to be the president who educates young children to the wonders of the world.

> ~ Lyndon Baines Johnson on the "Dignity of Man and the Destiny of Democracy," March 15, 1965

The quotes above are from two prominent U.S. presidents; one a Republican, the other a Democrat. Yet separate as they may be on policies, there is one point on which they converge: the dream of a respectful, personally and socially fulfilling society. This would be a society that encourages free-thinking, innovation, and inquiry but not at the expense of carelessness and abuse; a society that proceeds with due caution but not at the cost of growthful interchange among diverse people. It's an ideal, to be sure, but it's a peculiarly American ideal (at least as inspired by the Greeks and indigenous natives who fueled it). It is also a vision of the founders of the U.S. constitution, no matter how much they themselves tainted and perverted it throughout their epoch, and by implication epochs to come.

The ideal moreover is the great democratic (small "d")—republican (small "r") experiment that to this day inspires many, despite the corruption, ignorance, and forgetfulness of many of their leaders. The dream to support people to grow both emotionally and intellectually and to equip them for a flourishing society is also a core inspiration for this book. For *The Depolarizing of America* (and I use the latter term to mean "United States of America") is the culmination of years of effort to recognize the commonality of the aforementioned democratic–

republican visions, and to apply it to our contemporary crises—the crises of divisiveness and hate. It is also the culmination of years of experience with people who are sick and tired of their leaders speaking *for* them, and who wish to *speak for themselves* in terms of our democratic–republican ideals. Finally, the book recognizes, as will be elaborated later, that the American people have more in common than we tend to realize, and if we don't capitalize on that prospect, if we don't explore it through facing and talking with one another, we will surely squander it through civil discord or worse.

In this light, the book aims at two basic audiences—"everyday" people who seek to address social conflicts in their homes, neighborhoods, and communities; and professionals such as teachers, counselors, and organizational consultants who pursue conflict mediation in the more formal settings of schools, offices, and legislatures.

The book begins with some personal observations about our polarized state, both within the United States (and by implication) the world. It follows up with a reflection on how the sense of awe toward life—issuing in part from America's founding spirit--can serve as a counter to this polarized state. And it concludes with practical strategies centered on dialogue. These strategies translate awe-based sensibilities—humility and wonder toward life—to a rediscovery of one another, a rediscovery of our potential to heal.

The ideas discussed in this book, finally, are edgy, provocative, and potentially even revolutionary. Yet, if successful, these ideas will shake us out of our silos, bring us into genuine contact with one another, and return us to our founding vision—to "awe"-waken and mend the divides.

Introduction

The Awe for Life as a Basis for Democracy, Dialogue, and Renewal

The blocking of one's capacity for wonder and the loss of the capacity to appreciate mystery can have serious effects upon our psychological health, not to mention our whole planet.

~ Rollo May (1992, p, 5)

As of this writing, we are experiencing one of the largest pandemics the world has seen since the Spanish Flu. In this sobering light, the coronavirus 2019 moved the U.S. Surgeon General, Jerome Adams, to state: "We really need to lean into the health and safety of the American people. No more bickering, no more partisanship, no more criticism.... We all need to hit the reset button in moving forward for the health and safety of the American people" (Axelrod, 2020).

Adams has a point, of course—this *is* a time when we need to limit our bickering, move forward, and defeat the coronavirus. But it is also a time to be realistic. It will take more than a reset button to resolve that other "plague" to which Adams alludes—social polarization.

On a chilling scale, and throughout many parts of America and the world, people still hark to the drumbeat of strife: liberals bashing conservatives and conservatives trashing liberals; "Trumpers" deriding "Never Trumpers," and Never Trumpers slamming Trumpers; people of privilege debasing people of color and people of color counteracting people of privilege, particularly white privilege; men degrading women and women berating men; free-market capitalists demonizing social democrats and social democrats assailing free-market capitalists. There are abortion haters and abortion defenders, ardent secularists and absolute fundamentalists, unbowed nationalists and strident globalists. And there are even gut-wrenching divides about racial, ethnic, and political parties being responsible for the pandemic!

Now assuredly, there are many reasons for these splits in our society, ranging from economics to education to multiculturalism to the echo chambers of social media. Yet when all is said and done, there is one underlying layer that is not typically addressed—fear. When we fear we tend to fixate, we look for absolutes, and we reject competing points of view. Fear is the driver of polarization—the polarized mind— and it leads to "us/them," "black/white" thinking, feeling, and imagining. "If we can just keep our cherished view," many people contend, "if we can stick with what's familiar and routine, we will be okay." In the aftermath of 9/11, the recent upsurge in immigration, the onset of affirmative action, the loss of industrial sector jobs, the loss of status and tradition, and the loss of religious authority, many people turned Right and became more conservative. On the other hand, in the wake of the invasion of Iraq, the spate of gun violence, the surge of racism and sexism, and the criminality of profiteering, many people turned Left and became more liberal.

While it is true that some studies suggest that political conservatives tend to be more fearful and authoritarian than political liberals (e.g., see Kruglianski, Gelfand, & Gunaratna, 2012; Weir, 2019), this does not mean that the latter are exempt from such tendencies. Sometimes, in fact, as in the case of the French Terror, Stalinist Russia, and Maoist China liberals have also embraced fear-based and authoritarian political stances. The issue for many then appears to hinge on emotional reactivity as much or more than on political ideology (Zmigrod, Rentfrow, & Robbins, 2019).

The neglected layer of fear, moreover—and its resultant polarization—had long been a concern of our founders. They realized that fear was at the fount of tyranny, both liberal and conservative, and that a fearful people makes for a one-dimensional society, a society they toiled to escape in their native Europe. Hence, the antidote they proposed was to encourage people to grapple with their fears, to cultivate their own authority, and to risk the discovery, uncertainty, and experimentation that are at the fount of a democratic republic. Moreover, it was a belief that through embracing life's paradoxes— contrasts and contradictions—a people can grow. Not only can they grow in numbers but, even more significant, they can grow psychospiritually as a vital and multifaceted citizenry.

Indeed, a part of the founders' hope for America, as suggested by luminaries such as Jefferson and Adams, was that Americans could be comfortable enough with themselves to tolerate and even celebrate their differences with others, their discoveries with others. That the founders themselves fell contemptibly short of this vision does not taint its aspiration. It is a purview that encounters anxieties and finds within them new pathways and fresh possibilities. Hence Jefferson's remarks, historically situated as they may be, on the need for a broad and diversified education—for everyone: "I shall not die without a hope that light and liberty are on steady advance....And even should the cloud of barbarism and despotism again obscure the science and libraries of Europe, this country remains to preserve and restore light and liberty to them" (Lehman, 1985, p. 209).

Yet today, we seem woefully forgetful of this founding mandate. In far too many regions, we have lost touch with openness to learning and discovery and have devolved into fear-driven mobs and isolated groups. Uncannily, we have become more like what the founding revolutionaries fought against—closed and monolithic minds, battling tribes, and oppressed victims.

Hence, what we miss in this turbulence is a sensibility that most of us have heard about for our whole lives yet generally cast off to traditional religion or quips about extraordinary athletes or, increasingly, to corporate sloganeering. It is a sensibility that is too often highlighted in an ad or flashed on TV but is a much more nuanced and potentially life-changing sensibility than is generally recognized. What is the sensibility? Next to "love," "infinity," and "God," it is arguably the most far reaching and moving sensibility that we know— "awe."

Awe has been defined in many ways by many people over the millennia, and, as I suggest above, it was an impetus for our founding visionaries. Although awe began as a euphemism for "fear," it has gradually morphed into a mix of dread, veneration, and wonder. Moreover, awe became associated with the mysterious and powerful forces of nature and was considered the bedrock of most major religions—indeed the religious impulse itself. When Neolithic and perhaps even Paleolithic humans first experienced the roar of thunder, or the beating of rain, or the setting of the sun against the backdrop of great rocks and hills, or hordes of bison roaming the range, it is no great leap to infer that they experienced this quaking and quailing once equated with awe. In fact, as modern archeology has shown, this is precisely what the cave drawings of these early people suggest.

But gradually early humanity, and particularly their offspring, began to gather enough understanding and security toward their environs that they were able to experience them in a new light. Hence, instead of reflexively panicking and drawing back from the bewilderments of nature, they began to become curious about them, and this curiosity led to both theological explanations for them, such as perceiving them as byproducts of gods or a God, as well as more "rational" explanations, such as the predictable and measurable processes of creation. Yet the notion of the awesome as essentially inexplicable and unpredictable persisted, and so did its daunting scale. This worldview preserved the foundational *mystery* of awe but without the overriding emphasis on fear or terror in the wake of that mystery. At the same time, it also deepened the accompanying sensibilities of wonder, fascination, and even love for the dimension. Awe eventually became an equivalent to the element of the sublime in both literature and life. The basis for both religion and science but the captive of neither, awe increasingly became an outlook in itself, a feeling and sensation and cognition in itself. It became a term, both secular and theological, to describe a perception so vast that it could not fit any of the categories of our secular or even theological schemas, and so it was left as a formally vague yet experientially vital idea.

Today the sense of awe has become a "hot" topic both in the formal worlds of theology and science, as well as the less formal worlds of athletics, social media, and advertising. At the same time, though, I question whether these aforementioned areas really grasp the dynamism and transformative power of the topic or, equally, its radical implications for society. Either awe becomes associated with a belief about the properties of what some would call God, or it gets linked to the thrill and positivity of a beautiful scene in nature, an athletic event, or a charismatic personality. Yet these are fragments, in my view, which can be wonderful in themselves and as starters, but fail to capture the fullness and sublimity of the phenomenon: that fullness and sublimity have two major features—first, a daunting or *humbling* quality, and second, an intriguing or *wondering* quality. These humbling and wondering qualities form a rich tapestry of related aspects from dread to thrill and from veneration to boldness. The point, however, is that awe is a richly *paradoxical* experience, and we flirt with its extinction when we overemphasize either of its daunting or emboldening polarities.

Awe also has a life-changing component—as distinct from the momentary "high" or "fix"—that tends to be overlooked. Again, not to devalue such highs or fixes, they can be marvelous and indeed awe-inspiring when they arise. But too often they fade into compartmentalized flashes rather than life-altering realizations. Too often they devolve into individualized excitements rather than socially enduring virtues. I distinguish, therefore, between two types of awe. The first, the compartmentalized moments, I term—following an old

Japanese adage—the "quick boil" form of awe, and the second, the life altering or "slow simmer" form of awe. Again, both have their place, but it seems to me that these days we have an excess of the former and a dearth of the latter, and that the latter could help to revitalize our planet as well as individual consciousness.

To put it squarely, what I am talking about here is *the awe for life*, not just for parts of life. This sense of awe has the potential to transform every major sector of our lives, from the way we treat our fellow humans to our relationship to nature, to our engagements at work, to our deliberations in governance, to our freedom as individual and social beings. To be sure, and as previously indicated, awe has become a darling of the scientific research community. It is now seen in some quarters as more potent than happiness and is correlated with everything from increased feelings of love, generosity, and willingness to help others to decreased feelings of aggression and haste, and from increased religious and spiritual feelings to increased creativity, health, and life-satisfaction (Kaufman, 2018). The fact, however, is that awe— or what I have come to define as the humility and wonder, sense of adventure toward living—has a much greater reach than what has generally been established by conventional quantitative research. Qualitative inquiry, for example, has unveiled the profound implications of awe not only for the life transformation of individuals but also for the systems and structures they serve. Among these are experiences that energize pious and secularist alike, adults as well as children, ethicists as well as lawmakers. Moreover, the sense of awe can draw together the most divided thinkers, ideologues, and ethnicities; stretch across townships and cities, farmlands and seacoasts, countries and continents. It is an outlook that can nourish our environments, our bodies, and our intellects. How? Because awe embraces some of the foremost joys of the human journey—the excitement of learning, the exposure to new worlds and fresh possibilities, and the whole-bodied sense that one is alive and a part of something much greater than oneself.

Now, it may seem strange that the awe for life has something to do with democracy, but when looked at baldly, the connection is inescapable. As I will show in this book, awe (as I've defined it) is *foundational* to democracy. It is foundational to the value a democratic people place on life; the maturity level of such people; the meaning such people attain in their personal lives, which impacts the meaning people attain in their collective lives; and it is foundational to people's capacities for freedom—to wonder and to discover—as well as their capacities to support others' pursuit of freedom.

Correspondingly, the cultivation of awe for life can also serve as a check on democracy—namely, its potential excesses. Again, to the extent awe centers on life (existence) and not excessively on any person or part of life, it becomes a hedge against the fanaticisms and idolatries that have plagued democracies past. Moreover, by dint of its paradoxes—humility *and* wonder, thrill *and* anxiety—the awe for life is acutely attuned to human limitations and the need to be vigilant about those limits, lest awe mutates into presumption. In short, the awe for life is a basis for trust in people to run their own society and to curb their tendency to trust in false purveyors of awe, like leaders and institutions that promise the world but deliver illusions or worse, tyranny. To the extent that people are deficient in the awe for life, on the other hand, they are much more prone to be embittered, to feel desolate or numb and to project their hunger for spiritual connection on quick fixes, whether they be commercial products or leaders or mass movements. The net effect is the devaluation of life, the restriction of liberty, and the forfeiture of an enriched and dignified path.

On the pages to follow, accordingly, we will look at how the sense of awe toward life is mending divisions among individuals, cultures, and even political parties. We don't hear enough about these developments, but as a therapist and (sometime) social activist, I have observed them at close range and feel an urgency to describe them. It is in this way that others, similarly concerned, may find helpful tools in the battle for our depolarizing and democratic souls.

That said, there is an important caveat to bear in mind while reading this book: The dimension of awe is not always explicitly evident in the upcoming illustrations of dialogues. As with most sensibilities, people experience awe in degrees, and don't always express it overtly. On the other hand, I would contend that people's openness to the dialogues alone is an indicator of their humility and wonder or sense of adventure toward living—and this is what I anticipate many readers will feel as they tap into the offerings of this book.

I will begin then with my own awe-based healing, and how it may inform the healing of our times.

Suggested Readings and Resources

Axelrod, T. (2020). Media members react to "straight talk" from surgeon general. *The Hill,* March 14. Retrieved from https://thehill.com/homenews/media/487589-media-members-react-to-straight-talk-from-surgeon-general-quite-a-prescription.

Becker, E. (1973). *Denial of death.* Free Press.

Buber, M. (1958). *I and thou* (R.G. Smith, Trans.). Scribners.

Edsall, T. (2019, March). No hate left behind: Lethal partisanship is taking us into dangerous territory. *New York Times.* Retrieved from https://www.nytimes.com/2019/03/13/opinion/hate-politics.html.

Kaufman, S. B. (2018, November). Can you quantify awe? *Scientific American Blog Post.* Retrieved from https://blogs.scientificamerican.com/beautiful-minds/can-you-quantify-awe/.

Keltner, D., & Haidt, J. (2003). Approaching awe: A moral, spiritual, and aesthetic emotion. *Cognition and Emotion, 17,* 297–314.

Klein, E. (2020). *Why we're polarized.* New York, NY: Simon & Schuster.

Kruglianski, A., Gelfand, M., & Gunaratna, R. (2012). Terrorism as means to an end: How political violence bestows significance. In P. Shaver & M. Mikulincer (Eds.), *Meaning, mortality, and choice: The social psychology of existential concerns* (pp. 203–212). American Psychological Association Press.

Lehman, K. (1985). *Thomas Jefferson: American humanist.* University Press of Virginia.

Marcel, G. (2012). *The mystery of being.* Hard Press.

May, R. (1981). *Freedom and destiny.* Norton.

May, R. (1991). *The cry for myth.* Norton.

May, R. (1992). The loss of wonder. *Dialogues: Therapeutic applications of existential philosophy, 1,* 4–5 (a student publication of the California School of Professional Psychology, Alameda, CA).

McCullough, D. (2001). *John Adams.* Simon & Schuster.

Otto, R. (1923/1958). *The idea of the holy.* Oxford University Press.

Rokeach, M. (1961). *The open and closed mind.* Basic Books.

Schneider, K. (1990/1999). *The paradoxical self: Toward an understanding of our contradictory nature.* Humanity Books (distributed by Random House).

Schneider, K. (2013). *The polarized mind: Why it's killing us and what we can do about it.* University Professors Press.

Schneider, K. (2019). *The spirituality of awe: Challenges to the robotic revolution* (Revised ed.). University Professors Press.

Schneider, K., & Fatemi, S. (2019, April). Today's biggest threat: The polarized mind. *Scientific American Blog Post.* Retrieved from https://blogs.scientificamerican.com/observations/todays-biggest-threat-the-polarized-mind/

Weir, K. (2019, November). Politics is personal. *Monitor on Psychology.*
    Retrieved from https://www.apa.org/monitor/2019/11/cover-
    politics.
Wills, G. (2006). *Lincoln at Gettysburg: The words that reshaped America.*
    Simon & Schuster.
Zinn, H. (2003). *A people's history of the United States: 1492–present.*
    Harper Perennial.
Zmigrod, L., Rentfrow, P., & Robbins, T. (2019). The partisan mind: Is
    extreme political partisanship related to cognitive inflexibility?
    Journal of Experimental Psychology General, 149 (3). Retrieved from
    https://www.researchgate.net/publication/334984865_
    The_partisan_mind_Is_extreme_political_partisanship_related_to_cogn
    itive_inflexibility

Chapter 1

My Awe-Based Path to Dialogue

As sometimes happens with transformative experiences, the awe for life began for me with a tragedy. When I was almost three years old, my seven-year old brother died. I had no idea what hit me. All I knew was that my parents were sobbing, my brother was gone, and life before and after were like night and day. This upending of reality put me into a tailspin. I wet my bed constantly, I had night terrors, I went on crying jags (for what seemed like days), and I had explosive rage. At about four years old I was in such dire shape that I seemed to be losing touch with consensual reality. My world was filled with monsters, I was horrified of germs, and death seemed ever looming. My father, an educator, took notes on me. At this point I was much closer to terror toward life than awe.

Yet as distraught as they were, my parents had the foresight and sense of urgency to refer me to a child analyst (Dr. "S") when I was five years old! This was a tormenting time for me, but my analyst helped me to calm myself. His calmness and steadiness gave me a base from which to feel calmer and steadier myself. His ability to be present to me helped me to be more present to myself, to glimpse that I could survive the most horrific fears. As I reflect on it, Dr. S's presence helped me to enter a dimension that was bigger and more powerful than even death. This was the dimension of mystery. I realized that mystery eclipsed death because it is beyond anything that can be said or even felt about the state of being human. Mystery was the vast unknown, and the more that I learned to open to the unknown, the less I became paralyzed by fears and fantasies arising from my known world—the world of crying parents, helplessness, bodily threats, radical changes in my environment.

Gradually I was able to move from positions of abject terror to incremental intrigue and even wonder about the life that besieged me. I began to feel safer to open up to Dr. S. and to my parents. I began to feel a freedom well up in me, a sense that I could step back, collect my breath, and see more to my circumstances than absolute destruction and death. These realizations led me to look at scary movies with some degree of fascination vs. just simply paralyzing fright. I recall, for example being petrified by a late-night horror film called *The Cyclops* when I was about six years old. I was so braced by fear that night that I tore out of my friend's house (where I watched the film) and ran straight back to my house about half a block away. The wind was whipping and the air was frigid as I dashed, with racing heart, to my destination. The houses I passed looked downright evil, especially the one on the corner, with its peeling paint and dark windows. That was a traumatizing episode for me in many ways, which is partly why I recall it so vividly, and yet I felt a thrill about the episode, too. There was something of the amazing and fantastic about it, and my venture into the inky night air, the sense of something chasing me stirred me to wonder what that "monster" might know or reveal.

I had many such mixtures of fear and fascination walking up and down my street, looking at the puzzling houses, gnarled trees, and blowing leaves, particularly in the evening or when mesmerized by a fairy tale or show about the supernatural.

I think here of the many science fiction shows I watched, from "The Outer Limits" to "Twilight Zone" to "One Step Beyond" (a serial about the paranormal) and the chills yet thrills they brought to my awakening consciousness about life and the world. The theme that united many of these shows was a theme that united many of the facets of my psychological healing: a realization that the "alien," or "threat," or "monster" that appeared to be jeopardizing humanity (or my personal survival) was more like a messenger to an expanded consciousness. It was more like a shadowy guide unveiling a crisis that eventually might lead to a renewed understanding of life, the universe, or the unknown.

My encounter with such "alien" forms (or "forms of things unknown," as an Outer Limits episode was once titled), not only included traumatic loss but the environment in which I was brought up. I hailed from a secular Jewish family that had the pluck to root itself in a heavily Christian, working-class suburb of Cleveland, Ohio. This era was the late1950s, and although World War II had long ceased and the State of Israel was an inspiration to many, there was still a fair amount of bigotry in our neighborhood which showed up for me in a range of unnerving events. For example, one morning my parents and I woke up to find an enormous black swastika painted on the ping-pong table hanging in our garage. On several nightmarish occasions, I was called a "kike" and beaten up for being a Jew or having "killed Jesus"; I can't recall which, but either was repulsive enough. We had "greasers" and leather-clad motorcycle gangs in or near the neighborhood. Sometimes they also wore big crosses or the crosses of the German military, vintage World War II. I admired these characters in a strange way, and certainly took notice of their girlfriends, but I was also terrified of them, and astounded by their power, or what I took to be power.

There was also a time—probably several times—when I crossed over to the "demonic" side with the neighborhood bullies, and even bigots. Despite being reared on in-depth conversations about prejudice, politics, and "healthy societies," I buckled under a few times and joined the hateful masses. One of the most pivotal of these, which was also a turning point in my life, was the time I joined a gang of neighborhood kids who stalked a boy of color who was also what some considered "slow" mentally. I actually remember liking the kid and having sympathy for him because he was often picked on by callous peers. Yet here I was, one of those callous kids myself, chasing "Billy" down the street, calling him names and generally threatening him. I lost my conscience on that afternoon, and all I had been taught by my socially conscious parents. How this happened I'm not quite sure, as it was quite out of character for me. But it was most likely because I got particularly scared on that day—scared to oppose the crowd, the power of the closed mind, the smallness of being shunned.

In any event, in the middle of that abomination, my father abruptly ran up to me, pulled me out of the crowd, and spanked me hard for several seconds. This was extremely rare in itself, as my dad—and mom—practiced distinctly humanistic parenting skills, enabling me abundant room to express myself and to work through my own follies. But that afternoon was different—that action on my part was on a different plane, and my dad responded in kind; and I emphasize "responded" here because he didn't just react or explode. He not only used mild corporal punishment to send me a message, but he then sat me down and talked to me about the seriousness of my actions, expanding on how this must feel for Billy as well as how I would feel if I were him. And dad didn't stop there, as this incident became the springboard to an ongoing conversation about the toxicity of prejudice, and how we cut ourselves off from ourselves as much as from others in the process of debasing others. These ideas were already astir in our family environment growing up, but they became core, at least for me, from that time on.

That said, I must say that for all its alien "otherness," much of my experience of that neighborhood was life-affirming. Although there were kids to emphatically avoid, there were also several with whom I had a great time. This group continually played in the street together and on small but trimmed lawns or empty lots. We chased the ice cream truck together on sweltering summer days, met for Saturday afternoon movies, or made up our own skits, flipped baseball cards on Saturday afternoons, and joined in neighborhood cookouts.

I also had the chance to discover the charms of Christmas. My best friend had a tree every year, and I remember how fun it was to see presents around the tree, and to hear the Christmas stories. *A Christmas Carol* was one of my favorites, and I have a vivid memory of watching it with friends and at school. Christmas songs and television specials also had a spark for me. So here again was an illustration of the difference between abstract categories for the "other" (in this case Christians) and details "on the ground," so to speak, engaging living people, ideas, and actions. I also learned that Christianity could be about love and generosity as well as rejection and bullying.

My parents *talked to me* and opened me to the bigger picture of life. They used stories such as *Zorba the Greek, The Wizard of Oz*, and later films such as *To Kill a Mockingbird* and *Twelve Angry Men*, as object lessons in recognizing the humanity in marginalized people and the integrity it takes to open to that humanity. Slowly I began to see the many-sidedness of the people in my neighborhood and how, through talking, sports, and sharing holidays we could find some wondrous qualities in each other.

These were my early exposures to experiential democracy, or the challenge to grapple with mystery—the radical "other"—no matter how daunting. This led to my cultivation of freedom not only on the outside but on the inside too. Still, there is no doubt that this freedom, and eventual awe for life, came with a price. The price was anxiety, but it was also a healthy humility about how difficult it is to cultivate freedom, particularly if it is to endure. I learned the "slow simmer" approach to developing freedom, and the guardrails of anxiety have helped to focus it and highlight its opportunities. Yet none of this would have happened, I believe, without the parental and professional encouragement to stay open to mystery, no matter how daunting, along my rocky path.

My sense is that something of this experience was shared by the founders of our country, and I am not merely speaking of the famous leaders who presided over its formal emergence. I am also speaking of the legions of citizens who risked life and limb to develop a society that—for the privileged classes at least—enabled the unshackling of millennia of conditioning, both inner and outer, along with a renewed sense of how gratifying a fuller life could be. I have little doubt that this was the sentiment behind many of the slogans of the time such as "live free or die," and "we hold these truths to be self-evident, that all men are created equal, that they are endowed by their Creator with certain unalienable Rights...among these...Life, Liberty and the pursuit of Happiness." Moreover, I think this was the basic motive of Thomas Jefferson when he transformed the King James version of the New Testament into something closer to a secular guidebook for the humane and conscious life. There is humility and wonder—a sense of adventure toward living—shot through each one of these credos, and they express an enormous historically exceptional vision. It is a vision of trust, encounter, and deliberation.

Next, we consider the social consequences of this vision, some key ways that it shows up in our present times, and one of its most fruitful expressions: a citizen-inspired movement called the dialogue group.

Suggested Readings and Resources

Lehman, K. (1985). *Thomas Jefferson: American humanist.* University Press of Virginia.

Heschel, A. (1951). *Man is not alone: A philosophy of religion.* Strauss & Giroux.

Friedman, M. (1991). *Encounter on the narrow ridge: A life of Martin Buber.* St. Paragon House.

Roche, O. (Ed.). (1964). *The Jefferson bible: The life and morals of Jesus of Nazareth.*

Schneider, K. (2019). *Rediscovery of awe: Splendor, mystery and the fluid center of life.* Paragon House.

Schneider, K. (2019, November). The awe of being alive. *Aeon* online magazine. Retrieved from https://aeon.co/essays/to-feel-the-awe-of-living-learn-to-live-with-terror-and-wonder.

Chapter 2

Dialogue Groups for Everyday People

I believe that productive dialogue is something we should all be able to do. Even when we disagree. And if we can feel (heal the emotional part), it might keep us from going into the "attack back" mode and move ahead with love and respect.
~ Braver Angels workshop participant (Larson, 2020, p. 5)

As I write these words, I'm on a journey. Quite literally. I'm taking a train to a meeting in a modest urban walkup.[1]

Yet this is no ordinary meeting, and it is no ordinary day. I'm meeting a group called "Braver Angels,"[2] a grass-roots organization that has been sweeping the country over the last two years. As of January of 2020, Braver Angels had about 9,000 members in all 50 states and conducted nearly 1000 workshops with highly conflicting political partisans. Moreover, as of January 2020, Braver Angels amassed about 1300 volunteers to help coordinate its programs, workshops, and fundraising (Braver Angels Weekly Dashboard, February 2020). Specifically, the aim of Braver Angels is to bring Republican ("reds") together with Democrat ("blues") to simply speak to one another as opposed to bark and claw at one another through social media and public fights. But most important, the goal of Braver Angels is to help people with highly conflicting political views attempt to understand one another and see if there is any common ground. Braver Angels furthermore has a highly structured approach for this agenda. It

---

[1] The basic events described in this section are true, while some content has been altered to protect the confidentiality of those involved in the events.
[2] "Braver Angels" was originally named "Better Angels," but in April 2020 the organization decided to change its name to distinguish it from another group.

emphasizes respect for both the speaker and listener along with concerted exercises that help parties to "walk in each other's shoes," not to persuade or change each other's minds.

The goal again is to learn about and understand one another, with the strong likelihood that this will promote (at least some level of) common ground. But it cannot be forced. Heaven knows we've learned that through the (blood-stained) epochs.

So what was I doing spending three hours of my Saturday afternoon traveling into the city to connect with this mysterious assortment of virtual strangers, half of whom have completely contrasting political philosophies? And at a time when 11 worshipers at a Midwestern synagogue were just gunned down in cold blood for their religious affiliation and a prominent Republican representative had recently been shot and wounded for his political affiliation? How in the world do I think a group of 9 or 10 Braver Angels (including myself) will make one wit of difference in this crazy world, or have any measurable impact on the polarizing trend of our society?

It's because I believe in the awe for life, as I described in the last chapter, and this sensibility ties directly to a Braver Angels' dialogue. Indeed, it ties directly to any human relationship in the context of supporting its aliveness, its possibilities, and its participation in the remarkable drama of existence to the extent that is possible. And I not only found it possible, I found it tangible. I've sat in that group many times over the past two years and witnessed remarkable transformation.

I'd see the dark-haired fellow in the John Deere hat, and I'd think instantly of all those screaming partisans at the Trump rallies yelling "lock her up" or "U-S-A." Or then I'd hear, as I did on that Saturday afternoon, an angry therapist with yellowish shoulder-length hair bellow: "Now I want you 'Reds' (Republicans) in the group to explain to me why a man with an automatic weapon would go brazenly into a synagogue full of innocent people and open fire?!" While at first the group was stunned, one of the courageous "Reds" spoke up and yelled, "Foul! This is out of bounds. And while I understand that there are infuriated people here, I am offended that just because of my political affiliation I am linked to a weapon-carrying maniac!"

Slowly, others began to speak and the tone quickly shifted from one of accusation and blow-back to recognition of how far the altercation had strayed from our protocol. Cooler heads prevailed and brought us back to our basic mission, which was to sit with and learn from one another, not to demonize one another. This led to folks making room for the respective parties to explain their testiness that morning and to begin a healing process with one another. In the case of the accusatory Blue, this took the form of acknowledging that he had just experienced an anti-Semitic attack and could relate to the congregants at the Midwestern synagogue; and in the case of the offended Red, it took the form of expressing how unsafe the accusation made him feel, particularly because he experienced himself as a minority in a largely Blue community.

This episode impressed upon me the degree of courage, discipline, and dedication it takes to participate in a Braver Angels forum but also, on the other hand, the recognition that we *all* share such raw and reactive emotions from time to time. The question is can we learn from them and, like the feuding parties in this incident, acknowledge the context for our reactivity and find our way to a renewed colleagueship. The renewed colleagueship also struck me as a testament to the quality of facilitation in such meetings, and the structure, adherence to principles, and dedication that is encouraged.

Another experience I had in my Braver Angels group took place a few months later when a couple of new members showed up who had hailed, as I soon learned, from my hometown of Cleveland. One fellow was from a deep Red, rust-belt part of the area, and another from a decidedly Blue inner-city neighborhood. One fellow was white, the other black, and there I was from a quite different part of town observing them and myself in the process of observing. What I found was that although we came from sharply different walks of life, we gradually took a liking to one another. In fact, the commonality of geography was a strikingly cohesive factor, for what began as a cool and distant "getting to know one another" period as the group progressed concluded with the three of us huddled together reminiscing about our joys attending Cleveland Browns football games. We all homed in on the excitement of those early days in the '60s when running back Jim Brown was god and Gib Shanley and Jim Graner were sportscasting icons. But we didn't stop there, we then waxed nostalgic about the feel of the crowds in those days—the long march to Municipal stadium from the parking lots, the huge throngs of 80,000 plus all warming each other up with their steaming exhales and wafts of cigar smoke; the sense of anticipation, the great cultural and ethnic diversity; but, greatest of all for us, the sense of community those games brought. Those spectacles were one of the few—perhaps only!—times when Cleveland as a collective, rich and poor, middle class and working class, black and white all gathered together in a communal rite that brought warmth and good-heartedness above all to merging hordes. And what did the three of us see as we stepped back a moment and observed our close proximity, the half hour that had elapsed since the formal end of the group meeting, and the animation in our expressions? We saw—and felt—a group of motley guys, "strangers," who stood in wonder at the power of shared memories, poignant events, and unified communities; and we stood in awe of how the three of us had come together not only in physical proximity but in the proximity of our humanity and our definitive transcendence of stereotypes or labels.

This event reminds me that there are assuredly other group formats that can foster similar forms of mutuality, and they should be noted. For example, some formats provide a more elaborate and detailed approach to addressing race, class, and other social differences through formally crafted protocols (e.g., see Kim & del Prado, 2019; Sue, 2015). Others draw from the civil rights tradition such as the Community Healing Network's "Emotional Emancipation Circles" (Community Healing Network, 2018). These circles emphasize deep respect for African traditions of psychological liberation, from the indigenous practice of "Sawubona," which means "I see you" and "I see your humanity" to "culturally informing" and "culturally affirming" approaches "for persons of African ancestry to cope with... historical/persistent cultural trauma" (T. Jackson, personal communication, February 27, 2020). Still other groups utilize experiential tools such as mindfulness to facilitate multicultural healing (Magee, 2019). The issue here is to decide for oneself how one is willing to engage in group dialogue. For my part, the Braver Angels approach strikes a healthy balance between structure and informality, group process and individuality, although, as I suggest momentarily, I also think the Braver Angels format can be enhanced by a complementary approach that I call the Experiential Democracy Dialogue.

The Experiential Democracy Dialogue for Everyday People (Friends, Family, and Neighbors)

I will return to the Braver Angels format, and particularly their organization of workshops, later in this book but I will now describe what I have come to call the "Experiential Democracy Dialogue for Everyday People." This dialogue is a hybrid of what I have learned from my Braver Angels and other group approaches and a format that I developed years before those latter experiences. Specifically, the Experiential Democracy Dialogues differ from the Braver Angels' approach in three basic ways. First, the former is a one-on-one encounter, whereas the latter (with one exception I'll address) comprises groups. Second, the former is a less formally structured approach that can be used by most anyone with a basic level of maturity and willingness to work through a cultural, political, or religious conflict with another person, whereas the latter generally requires a highly structured format with trained facilitators (moderators). Third, the former evokes an intimacy and depth that is sometimes difficult to achieve in the group format but that can serve as a supplement to or follow up from the latter. That said, I have seen how the two formats can work together and are mutually reinforcing on the path to a more civil and enlightened society.

Let me begin then with the most basic and, I believe, broadly applicable Experiential Democracy Dialogue format. I call this "the Experiential Democracy Dialogue for Everyday People" because this is a format for the ordinary (comparatively composed) person who struggles with social, cultural, and political conflicts every day and yet has few means to address or resolve them. This is also a dialogue for people who contend with such conflicts among families, neighbors, and fellow citizens and yet who are open to addressing them. (For a sample of potential dialogue topics, see pp. 72-73).

I envision the Experiential Democracy Dialogue for Everyday People as a supplement or follow-up to the group dialogues of Braver Angels (or like-minded) organizations. Although it is best guided by a reasonably mature and stable facilitator, it does not require such a facilitator, particularly if it involves two people who are dedicated to the ground rules and adhere to timelines.

My hope is that because of the comparatively simple, safe, and basic nature of this style of dialogue, it will be adopted by a significant number of people. These are people who share a profound concern for the alarming rates of division and strife in our country and the world at large. They are also people who experience this strife in their families, among friends, and even in love relationships. Few today are untouched by these upheavals, and many, I contend, would relish a chance, difficult as it may be, to at least begin a process of mending wounds.

This process may be even more compelling today in the wake of the coronavirus (COVID-19). As people realize the degree to which divisiveness and hate erode rather than promote the welfare of all, there is an opening for greater efforts at civility and the search for common ground. These efforts can in turn lead to a greater receptivity to the Experiential Democracy Dialogue, but with certain realistic safeguards. These safeguards center on the management of understandable anxieties associated with COVID-19—particularly in the early phases of recovery—and can be elaborated as follows: First, the dialogue may need to be carried out at a social distance (i.e., 6 feet apart, and possibly with masks); second it may need to be conducted in a spacious and sanitized setting, such as a home or a sizeable office; and third, if appropriate (e.g., for classrooms, community meetings, or older populations), it may need to be conducted online via a reliable video platform. Although the latter alternative is limited, it has nevertheless been shown to be a fruitful complement to or even, if necessary, a replacement for "live" encounters (see Braver Angels, 2020).

The experiential democracy dialogue for everyday people therefore begins with the following set of guidelines.

The first task is to *read and adhere to* the **Ground Rules.** These ground rules have been adapted from the Braver Angels (2019a) Comprehensive Moderator Guide. The ground rules are as follows:

1) *The point of this dialogue is to understand and learn about each other; not to convince anyone or change their mind.*
2) *Please speak for oneself and not for another person or party. The point is to explain one's view to another person or to listen to them, not to accuse them, presume their point of view, or assume the point of view of some outside group.*
3) *Agree to stick to the spirit of the activities designed for each phase of the dialogue. For example, if the topic is what we each learned from listening to one another that's all we adhere to, even if it means resisting the urge to explain our own cultural or political view.*
4) *The rest is pretty standard—taking turns, not interrupting the other, listening carefully and mindfully to the other, respecting the other's attempt to convey their view, (e.g., no eye-rolling or loud sighs when the other is speaking). In other words, bringing our best selves to a difficult conversation.* (p. 30)

The second task is to agree to the **Goals and Principles** of the dialogue, which are adapted again from Braver Angels (Skills Workshop Presenters' Guide, 2019b, p. 5). These goals and principles are:

1) *Abandon Expectations*
   • Of changing the other's core beliefs and attitudes

- That facts will be agreed on, and logic will be followed consistently
- That your conversation partner will match your openness

2) *Follow the Core Principles*
  - That respect, curiosity, and openness tend to elicit the same from the other person
  - That everyone needs to save face—and that no one is portrayed as stupid, blind, narrowly self-serving, or bigoted
  - That most people in a relationship have common values and concerns that can be unearthed

3) *Adhere to the Following Cautions*
  - Start at a calm moment, not after someone has fired off a verbal shot or is in mid-rant
  - Only try this dialogue with someone you think might want to hear your point of view
  - To the extent possible, engage this dialogue (as well as all those described in this book) in a "living" face-to-face context and not one that is remote or electronically mediated

4) *Remember the Following Four Skill Sets:*
  - Set a constructive tone, meaning draw from a perspective of genuine curiosity rather than one of entrapping or belittling; remember that it's not just what you say but *how* you say it that can have the largest impact
  - Listen in a way that the other person feels heard. For example, take a position of humility; make every effort to "put yourself in the other's shoes"; paraphrase the other's essential points when called for
  - Speak in a way that helps the other person hear you. For example, use "I" statements to describe positions vs. speaking for outside parties or assuming the mantle of objective truth; acknowledge your potential for short-sightedness; recognize that you're speaking to a person and not a stereotype
  - Be ready to handle difficult moments, such as hostility or attacks by avoiding likeminded reactions, reminding one's partner of the ground rules, maintaining one's composure and proceeding with the format or, if necessary, exiting the situation until it is less heated

Five Phases

The first phase of the Experiential Democracy Dialogue for Everyday People is **Visualizing Encounter with the Other.** Visualizing encounter with the other is a "warm-up" phase in which the conflicting parties separately and in a safe space, take 5 to 10 minutes to visualize what it may be like to just simply sit with the other and discuss the issue that has been selected (e.g., the issue can be any point of cultural, religious, or political conflict that the parties choose to address). What thoughts, feelings, or images arise in the presence of the culturally, religiously, or politically different other with whom you are about to encounter, and can you manage them? For example, does the other bring back a difficult memory, such as an argument or heated debate? Or perhaps the encounter conjures up a feeling of being tense or uncomfortable, angry or irritable. See if you can take a few moments to acknowledge this but then put those feelings aside in the interest of curiosity, discovery, and furthering the cause of a personally and socially gratifying society alluded to earlier in this book.

That said, it should be noted that this exercise, as all exercises contained in this book *should be aborted* if there is any sense that one is overwhelmed by or unable to engage in the task at hand. It should also be noted that if the disagreement is so serious as to jeopardize a close relationship or one's emotional stability, the parties or party concerned should consult a mental health professional to help them work through the issue.

After identifying thoughts, feelings, or images associated with the imagined encounter with the other, see if you can collect your breath, and again find a place of centeredness with the issues that arise—a place where you can acknowledge some discomfort but be okay with proceeding.

At the point at which the parties find a place of relative composure while experiencing the visualization, then they are ready to meet for the aforementioned dialogue. To better support this dialogue, a third person can be asked to be the facilitator. Again, this facilitator does not need to be a professional or expert in human relations, but he or she does need to agree to the ground rule of neutrality. That is, the facilitator, who could be a friend or family member needs to be able to remain as impartial as possible in order to maximize the abilities of the conflicting parties to feel 1) safe, 2) free to express their personal opinions, and 3) able to constrain themselves to attempting to understand and learn about the other party rather than engage in accusation, devaluation, or imposition of their view on the other party. It cannot be stressed enough that these ground rules are vital for meaningful engagement with the other. They also enhance the prospect for the achievement of a common ground between the two parties, which is a potential pathway to healing both their particular relationship as well as that of others in the community. Finally, the facilitator is helpful to ensure that the participants adhere to the time limits of each phase; this can be done by the participants themselves but it makes their task a bit more difficult.

Once the participants in the dialogue are ready, they are then invited to engage in the balance of the five-phase process. There is always a speaker and a listener during these timed phases. The listener must refrain from any speaking or interference while the speaker is talking, and the speaker, per the ground rules, agrees to be respectful and delimited to making "I-statements" as opposed to speaking for others including their partner.

This second phase then is the **Background Phase**, which is allotted 15 minutes. This phase begins with the facilitator (or one of the conversation partners) asking one of the parties to "Briefly describe what it was like for you to grow up, focusing in particular on aspects of your environment and upbringing that pertain to the issue at hand." For example, if the issue at hand is immigration, then the partner is asked to describe how their family or caretakers viewed immigration, taxing the rich, and so on. Then after five minutes, the facilitator asks that same party to "Briefly expand on how the political, cultural, or religious 'other' or outgroup was treated by your family viewpoint." (The characterization of the "other" must pertain to the political, cultural, or religious "other" with which the parties are in conflict. Therefore, if the theme of the dialogue is a disagreement about race, then the party speaking describes how race was treated in their family and cultural background; if it's about politics, then the same process is carried out). The process is then reversed so that the speaker is now the listener and the listener is now the speaker.

The third phase, **Turn-taking a Stance**, is the facilitation of 5 minutes for each dialogue partner to tell (as mindfully and heartfully as possible) his/her "side" of an issue that brought him/her to this meeting. At the end of the 5 minutes, the listening partner is asked to reflect back to the speaking partner what he/she understood the speaking partner to convey. This feedback aspect should be engaged in with one's whole bodily experience (thoughts, feelings, intuitions) as to what the speaking partner attempted to convey. It is an exercise in the attempt to understand and, to the degree possible, suspend judgment about the viability of the speaking partner's point of view. Following this feedback, the speaking partner is then given the chance to correct or clarify any perceived shortcomings (gaps) in the listening partner's paraphrasing of him/her, so that all efforts are made to capture the speaking partner's intended meanings. This part of the phase should take about 3 minutes. The roles are then reversed so that the speaking partner is now the listener and the listening partner is now the speaker, following the same format as above.

The fourth phase is **Identifying and Correcting Stereotypes.** This phase has proved critical as a way for each dialogue partner to register their concerns with how they've been caricatured (concerning the particular issue at hand) but also with regard to humbling themselves when identifying the kernels of truth in those stereotypes. The exercise, which derives from the Braver Angels workshop format, proceeds as follows: The partners rotate again so that the first speaker in the last exercise now takes 3–5 minutes to describe how he or she has been stereotyped for their position; this speaker then takes about 3–5 minutes to correct (or show what is false and misleading about) the way they've been stereotyped. Finally, the first speaker takes 2 minutes to identify the nuggets of truth to the way they've been stereotyped. The partners then rotate so that the first speaker then becomes the listener and the initial listener now becomes the speaker. The net effect of this exercise is that dialogue partners become more "human" to each other as they both rise above and transcend simplistic conceptions about themselves and also show their susceptibility to sometimes being problematic, or possibly even offensive and hateful. When the respective dialogue partners can witness this complexity and vulnerability in each other, it can often lead to a greater sense of commonality, or at least accessibility, as the reflection about each other deepens.

The fifth phase is **Discovery and the Prospect for Common Ground.** This is the final phase in which the parties each have 10 minutes to disclose what, if anything, they learned about each other, and if there is a prospect for common ground or action. This phase is particularly important for the future direction of the participants involved, and the question as to whether they see new ways to view each other, the conflicting partisans in their everyday lives, and the needs of the country. It is also a chance to consider action steps the respective parties may take in the wake of their encounters.

Note: As a follow-up to this exercise or for dialogue partners who are particularly skilled at working with each other, the above format can be modified to add a **Question Phase** to the format. The Question Phase, which also draws from the Braver Angels workshop format, would follow the Stereotype exercise and proceed as follows: Each participant is invited to ask respectful, honestly searching questions that promote respectful, honestly deliberative responses. An example of this Question Phase might be "How do think your view is good for the country?" Or "Help me understand how you came to value issue X or leader Y?" Or "Do you have any concerns about your view on X?" This form of inquiring is an art and should be engaged in with care. The same rules apply to these questions as to earlier interchanges—no interrupting while the other party is speaking, maintain a curious and composed disposition (vs. a disposition of irritability, impatience, or condescension), and avoid "gotcha" questions or questions that assume the answer in the question.

For a handy summary of the Experiential Democracy Dialogue for Everyday People, see Table 1 below.

Table 1
Experiential Democracy Dialogue for Everyday People
Summary of Phases

- **Phase 1—Visualization of Engaging in a Dialogue with One's Partner**: Facilitation of the thoughts, feelings, and fantasies that emerge when meditating on engaging in dialogue with ones' partner. This is a warm-up phase that may or may not be necessary, given comfort level and/or time constraints for the exercise. Note: Occasionally visualizations may have the effect of creating more anxiety than initially experienced for this exercise. If that is the case, or if either party experiences excessive anxiety of any kind, the exercise should be suspended until or if a reasonable degree of comfort is attained.

- **Phase 2—Background**: Facilitation of 5 minutes for each dialogue partner to tell very briefly about what it was like to grow up in their family/community context and how outgroups or "cultural others" were treated.

- **Phase 3—Turns Taking a Stance**: Facilitation of 5 minutes for each dialogue partner to tell (as mindfully and heartfully as possible) his/her "side" of an issue that brought them to this encounter. The listening partner then reflects back what he/she heard, and the speaking partner corrects any gaps in the feedback. This latter engagement should take about 3 minutes.

- **Phase 4—Identifying and Correcting Stereotypes**: Turn-taking identifying perceived stereotypes of one's particular side, correcting those views, and identifying nuggets of truth to them; 5 minutes each party.
- **Phase 5—Discovery and Prospect for Common Ground**: 5 minutes each. Facilitation of turn-taking on what was discovered: for example, Did the partner feel heard? Did the partner relate to the story? What was learned? Any potential for common ground, action steps?[3]

In summary, the Experiential Democracy Dialogue for Everyday People is intended to "give away" key skills and resources. These skills and resources, sparked by an awe toward life, have been found successful in more formal settings but they need not be confined to formal settings. Moreover, while the Experiential Democracy Dialogue for Everyday People is not a replacement for formal settings, it can be fruitful in its own right, extending the power of dialogue to homes and communities. Finally, for those dialogue partners who are interested, the format outlined in this chapter can be repeated. These repetitions can involve the original dialogue partners, in which case each partner's respective viewpoints can be deepened and clarified, or the format can be extended to new dialogue partners, which may enhance the general environment for all concerned. In either case, the idea here is to expand the network of dialogues, deepen the bonds of communities, and to enhance the representation of government.

Suggested Readings and Resources

Bellah, R., Madsen, R., Sullivan, M., Swidler, A., & Tipton, S. (1985). *Habits of the heart: Individualism and commitment in American life.* Perennial Library.

Braver Angels (2019a). Proposed ground rules. From the *Comprehensive Moderator Guide*, 8. 2019. Braver Angels.

Braver Angels (2019b). *Skills workshop presenters' guide.* Braver Angels.

---

[3] As noted above, for bolder or more skilled participants, a Questions Phase can be engaged following the Stereotypes Phase. Then proceed to the "Discovery and Prospect for Common Ground" Phase.

Braver Angels (2020). What we do. Retrieved from
    https://braverangels.org/what-we-do/
Bridging the Divide (2020). Glide Memorial's community healing project.
    Retrieved from https://www.glide.org/church/bridging-the-divide/.
Carson, C. (2002). *A call to conscience: The landmark speeches of Dr.
    Martin Luther King Jr.* Grand Central Publishing.
Community Healing Network (2018). *Emotional emancipation circles.*
    Retrieved from https://www.communityhealingnet.org/emotional-
    emancipation-circle/.
Kim, A.S., & del Prado, A. (2019). *It's time to talk (and listen): How to have
    constructive conversations about race, class, sexuality, ability & gender
    in a polarized world.* New Harbinger.
Larson, C. (2020). *Experiential liberation within the socio-political divide: A
    phenomenological qualitative analysis of encounters with the liberal or
    conservative other.* [Manuscript in preparation]. Sponsored by the
    Fielding Institute, Santa Barbara, CA under a grant from the Kristine
    Mann Psychoanalytic Institute.
Magee, R. (2019). *The inner work of social justice: Healing ourselves and
    transforming our communities through mindfulness.* Tarcher-Perigee.
Pearson, G. (2011) African famine: "I see you." *Huffington Post,* October
    9. Retrieved from https://www.huffingtonpost.ca/glen-
    pearson/africa-famine_b_922063.html?guccounter=1 . [Discussion of
    "sawubona"]
Schneider, K. (2016, March). The experiential democracy project: A depth
    approach to the legislative process. Retrieved from
    https://www.madinamerica.com/2016/03/experiential-democracy/.
Schneider, K. (2018, October). Awe trumps polarization. *The
    Hermeneutic Circular*, pp. 32–34. (A publication of the Society for
    Existential Analysis. Retrieved from https://existentialanalysis.org.
    uk/wp-content/uploads/2019/11/2018-October.pdf).
Sue, D. W. (2015). *Race talk and the conspiracy of silence: Understanding
    and facilitating difficult dialogues on race.* Wiley.

Chapter 3

The Experiential Democracy Dialogue for Schools and Classrooms

With so many layers of cultural, political, and religious conflict in our society, it is no wonder that such problems reverberate in our nation's schools. In fact, classrooms have become hotbeds of intersectional controversy, from issues of race, to gender and sexual orientation, to political affiliation, where everyone from teachers and administrators to students reel from their charge. But such difficulties may not be sound bases to censor potentially educative conversations. In fact, the inclination to ban such conversations, which appears to be gathering momentum in certain quarters, contradicts the basic spirit of inquiry (awe-based consciousness) that many see as integral to education (Lukianoff & Haidt, 2018). Given this state of affairs, the Experiential Democracy dialogue may be a comparatively safe, appropriately structured, and enlivening way to redress the problem.

Specifically, the Experiential Democracy Dialogue can be used for a variety of classroom formats. Whenever the focus is on cultural, political, or religious differences and students have attained the requisite maturity, this dialogue can be fruitful. Again, to the extent that students do not seem ready for this dialogue or feel overwhelmed, the dialogue should either be avoided or supported by a mental health professional who can help the student(s) work through the difficulty. Among the suggested settings for this dialogue may be upper level sociology, psychology, or civics classes in high school and classes in sociology, psychology, international relations, political science, philosophy, anthropology, and history in college or graduate school. I myself have used this approach with counselors and psychotherapists who are interested in applying their mediation skills to broader social conflicts than those with whom they work in their clinics or offices.

Generally, I have found Phase 1—visualization of what it might be like to engage in dialogue with a person of a contrasting disposition—

to be a very rich opening to this exercise. Sometimes it can even invoke a sense of awe.

After suggesting to students that they close their eyes and begin to "look" inward, this phase can be elaborated with prompts for students to "stay present" to the thoughts, feelings, and body sensations of encountering a social "other." As students do so, I often find that the exercise enlivens their discoveries both about themselves and the socially conditioned images they have about diverse lives. For example, I've had politically liberal students picture sitting with politically conservative students, and vice versa, and discover that just the thought of such "others" triggers memories of tension, and sometimes even great frustration sitting with (in this case) conservative parents, grandparents, and other relatives. This tension and frustration often takes the form of a resignation about how to resolve the situation—or it devolves into name-calling and accusation.

Yet one of the beauties of this dialogue process is that it provides a chance for students (or anyone) to begin to reassess what it may be like to engage in the encounter differently, within safer boundaries, and with a more curious attitude. Such an opportunity shifts into full gear when I take students through one or two subsequent phases—like asking them to picture how they might feel to hear the other express what it was like for them to grow up (Phase 2) and how their caretakers treated outgroups (such as liberals) in the family system. Or what it might be like for students to hear the other express their stance with them while they attempted to understand that stance as fully and mindfully as possible; and, conversely, what it might be like for them to picture themselves telling the other about their own story and how outgroups were treated. Again, it's the structure of the exercise that helps to create the sense of safety both in hearing about the other and enabling the other to hear about oneself. For example, one student might imagine her crusty old granddad really begin to open up and talk about what it was like for him as a child during the Great Depression when he had to scramble for food and basic necessities, and how he had to get menial jobs just to put bread on his family's table. Or the student might picture how the grandfather would resent government handouts for able-bodied people who chose not to work but whom he nevertheless had to support. Or how he would complain about the lack of religious morals "these days" and that the bloodiest wars in the 20th century were perpetrated by secular men, and so on. That student would then imagine paraphrasing what she heard from this man, with as much openness and compassion as she can muster. She would picture herself relating her background story and stance, and picturing him doing his best to feed back to her what he heard, with as much openness and compassion that he could muster.

It wasn't that students would begin changing their values based on these imagined exchanges, or even perhaps their distaste for the abstract viewpoints which they represented. But what did seem to happen is that students gradually began to see—and, more important, feel—the genuine person behind the viewpoints and the context out of which that person brought his concerns. A number of the students also realized more about how they themselves were triggered by the views of the imagined other, and by reexamining those triggers in the light of the *person* with whom they were interacting (whether real or imagined) began to shift somewhat in their assessment of that person. The person, in short, began to become more than the assemblage of stereotypes and media images that the student may have begun with, and could increasingly be seen as one who might be understood, and possibly even resonated with, even if the basic value differences remained. This was a start, and for many a basis on which to begin the exercise in earnest, either with another student who genuinely held an opposing view, or one who held similar views but was willing to embody (role-play) a social other so that the exercise could be fully engaged. Either way, the results of these encounters were almost invariably illuminating to the students, helping them to discover notable dimensions of themselves as well as others for whom they had held deep resentments or prejudices.

Hence, my suggested framework for this exercise is as follows: 1) Introduce students to the idea of the Experiential Democracy Dialogue, along with the caveat that participation in the Dialogue is strictly voluntary and that anyone should feel perfectly free to opt out if unduly disconcerted by it; 2) invite them to visualize what it might be like to sit with and encounter, in the manner of the Dialogue format, a social (cultural, political, religious) "other" (visualization of one or two of the phases should suffice here); 3) invite them to discuss and process what they experienced in that visualization; 4) invite them to then begin the exercise with an actual partner in the class, guiding and timing the pairs through each of the subsequent four phases—background, stance, perceived stereotypes toward their stance, followed by correction of those stereotypes and the kernels of truth to those stereotypes—with an optional questions phase; and finally 5) invite students to discuss what they discovered about themselves and the other from the exercise, followed by a discussion of whether there was any common ground or basis for action steps in the world.

On a final note, this version of the Experiential Democracy Dialogue should optimally be carried out by a classroom instructor with some background in group or interpersonal mediation (which by dint of their specialty many instructors possess). The instructor should also carefully read through this book, as well as some of the material on websites like Braver Angels. While the instructor does not need to be a formally trained professional in group mediation and dialogue, he or she should remain acutely vigilant about the depth and degree of his/her skill in this dialogue process and square that skill with the extent and depth of the exercises described in this section. Generally speaking, the classroom format is not a place for intensive or lengthy engagement of the dialogue process, and that is why I recommend the visualization phase and perhaps a select few others for this format. However, even one or two of the phases can give students a substantive "taste" of the dialogue process, and what it may imply for the future of their social interactions as well as those of the society around them.

Suggested Readings and Resources

Lukianoff, G., & Haidt, J. (2018). *The coddling of the American mind: How good intentions and bad ideas are setting up a generation for failure.* Penguin.

Heterodox Academy. (Website for constructive discussion of political differences in academia. Retrieved from https://heterodoxacademy.org/

PsychAlive (2014). Dr. Kirk Schneider on psychological and cultural polarization. (Interview by L. Firestone). *Glendon Foundation* productions. Retrieved from https://www.youtube.com/watch?v=-J144StwlBw.

Schneider, K. (2009). *Awakening to awe: Personal stories of profound transformation.* Jason Aronson.

Schneider, K. (2013). *The polarized mind: Why it's killing us and what we can do about it.* University Professors Press.

Chapter 4

The Experiential Democracy Dialogue with Professional Facilitation

A great relationship...throws a bridge from self-being to self-being across the abyss of dread...
~ Martin Buber (1955, p.175)

This version of the Experiential Democracy Dialogue is designed for organizations or people who require more formal guidance in the implementation of their encounters. For example, this approach was originally designed to assist legislators to enhance their capacity to resolve policy debates during the George W. Bush administration. This was a time, not unlike today, when lobby-driven rhetoric, entrenched ideologies, and politically inflamed crises (such as the Iraq war, hate crimes, and increasing class conflict) too often fostered hurt-filled bickering rather than curiosity-filled deliberation. I made several efforts to facilitate this form of the Experiential Democracy Dialogue to legislators at the time but was mostly met with responses such as "great idea but, I just can't risk my political career on this"; "The positions are too entrenched and the voters are in no mood for evolving points of view"; "The legislators themselves are too polarized, and none would authentically participate."

While I recognized the kernels of truth in many of these reactions, I also felt irked by them. My overall feeling was that if legislators, who hold some of the most fateful decisions of our lives in their hands, are not even willing to attempt these kinds of dialogue, how or why would anyone else make such an effort? And if leaders don't lead, then how will crises ever get substantively addressed? Still, I adamantly hoped that someone would take a risk—if not for themselves, then for the sake of our democracy—and potentially spark a chain of like-minded engagements. Yet with the exception of some very friendly and even appreciative encounters with certain legislators, my efforts fell on deaf ears.

Today, however, we may be in even greater need for such "person-to-person" meetings, and because of groups like Braver Angels, the attempts to facilitate them will perhaps be more persuasive to such leaders.[1] This at least is my hope with this book and in the work I continue to pursue. Moreover, I frankly admit that legislators aren't the only ones who are intimidated by these experiential dialogues; I too have been struck by their capacity to make people in any walk of life feel jarred at times—or even worse, unsafe. Therefore, it is in that light that I, as indicated earlier, have modified the formats of the dialogues. They are now designed to feel safer, less free-wheeling, and more psychologically contained. Hence, it is my sincerest wish that this revised approach, this experiment in social healing, will have a new appeal today and that a few courageous lawmakers will sample it.

That said, both older and newer forms of the professionally facilitated Experiential Democracy Dialogue have been successfully engaged in with practitioners in the fields of counseling and clinical psychology, nursing and medicine, and police and community activists (as illustrated below). I have also worked with the approach internationally and found great interest among students and professionals in the field of mental health. Finally, the professionally facilitated format may be helpful to "everyday" people who feel too daunted by the idea of conducting the dialogues on their own, or with the assistance of laypersons in the community.

The professionally facilitated Experiential Democracy Dialogue entails a modified version of the five (and optionally six) phases discussed earlier, but with the addition of a trained facilitator (or moderator) who can help support and deepen the process. The qualifications for such facilitators are that they have at least a post-graduate degree in mental health counseling or psychotherapy *and* that they have participated in and facilitated at least one Experiential Democracy Dialogue themselves. Although such training opportunities have heretofore been quite limited, my hope is that with the advent of this book more such opportunities will arise, and along with them the emergence of professional facilitators who initiate the dialogues on their own.

---

[1] One of the cofounders of Braver Angels, Bill Doherty, has already begun to use the Braver Angels group format with a group of legislators. See the Braver Angels website (www.braverangels.org) for more information on this development.

The first and most important aspect of the professionally facilitated Experiential Democracy Dialogue is who is being facilitated and what is their aim? If the parties involved are two family members for example, the facilitator will need to modify the approach to consider the context and needs of these two family members. If the parties are in a classroom or a large group, a different set of factors will come into play. In the latter instance, for example, the facilitator could give a demonstration of the approach (along with power point slides that allow audience members to follow along) and then invite audience members to pair up and try the process themselves. Depending on the purposes of the organization or group, they could role play their encounters or they could work with real-life differences in their pairs. Ideally, the professional facilitator will be able to utilize other professional facilitators to work with each pair, but short of that they could assign members of the audience to facilitate simpler or more structured dialogues to work with the pairs. The professional facilitator would then play the role of overseer to help the lay facilitators as needed with each respective pair. The upshot, however, is that these professionally facilitated groups would end up in triads—the dialogue partners and a facilitator who is overseen and coordinated by the lead professional facilitator.

Hence, the professionally facilitated dialogue should roughly follow the same format as discussed earlier for the Experiential Democracy Dialogues for Everyday People, except with minor modifications in time and depth of interchange as the lead facilitator sees fit. That said, here's a rough format that could be followed: The first phase, **Visualizing One's Dialogue Partner,** would take roughly 5–10 minutes total; the second phase, describing one's **Background**, and how one's caretakers treated culturally, politically, or religiously different "others" (depending on the topic selected) should take approximately 15 minutes total; the third phase **Taking a Stance** should take about 15 minutes total; the fourth phase—naming, correcting, and acknowledging the nuggets of truth in perceived stereotypes—should take about 20 minutes total; the fifth phase, **Asking Respectful Question(s)** of one's partner, should take about 15 minutes total; and the sixth phase, **Discovery and Common Ground,** should take about 15 minutes total. This adds up to a grand total of just under 90 minutes, which along with audience questions could amount to a two-hour workshop.

It should be noted that with professionally facilitated dialogues there is somewhat more room for elaboration of feelings about topics discussed; the main point, however, is that it is incumbent on the lead facilitator to ensure that whatever deepening processes occur do so within the basic ground rules of the encounter. Hence, while a more experiential dialogue is supported in the professionally facilitated format, it still must be delimited by respectful, comparatively composed, and open-minded exchanges between dialogue partners, and this must be artfully monitored.

Ideally, these professionally facilitated dialogues can be the basis of a series of follow-up dialogues or can be complements to the group processes engaged in the Braver Angels dialogues. The basis for this approach is that, anecdotally, the more that people have an opportunity to elaborate on and deepen their dialogues, the more they seem to feel that such dialogues have a lasting impact on their perceptions of social otherness and thereby on their actions in the world; whereas brief or single-episode dialogues have sometimes been found to be superficial for participants and delimited with regard to their effects on actions such participants take in the world.

Illustration: An Experiential Democracy Dialogue on Community Policing

The following is a lightly edited transcript of a professionally facilitated Experiential Democracy Dialogue. The dialogue took place in March of 2016 at the Society for Humanistic Psychology Conference, San Francisco State University. Prior to the conference, I asked an African American colleague and community activist, Nathaniel Granger, and a Caucasian police officer, Rodger Broome, to engage in an Experiential Democracy Dialogue as I facilitated their encounter with the topic of community policing, and they gladly agreed. Nathaniel and Rodger were both mental health professionals in addition to their other roles exhibited in the dialogue, and they both had prior acquaintance with each other. This latter point is important because it means that these two dialogue partners may not be representative of partners who are completely unknown to each other. On the other hand, the connection between Nathaniel and Rodger represents the value of an established relationship in the effective facilitation of intensive dialogues between people of diverse backgrounds. This, too, is important because there are many such established relationships among families, friends, and members of communities who are also in conflict and who may similarly benefit.

That is not to say that such dialogues cannot be carried out between strangers, but it does suggest a note of caution when applying such intensive procedures in other forums where people have little or no knowledge of each other. In the latter case, for example, a lengthier familiarization process may be called for, along with a heavier emphasis on safety and structure.

The video version of the dialogue between Nathaniel and Rodger is available on YouTube (https://www.youtube.com/watch?v=g92cNF5-Tpw), but for the purposes of this book I present it, with minor editing, below. In my view, the text is valuable both for its detailed representation of the dialogue format and its timely illumination of the charged and challenging topic of community policing. To my knowledge, this dialogue marks one of the rare occasions on which an African American activist and a White police officer meet for the express purpose of learning about and attempting to understand each other. The intimacy and depth of the meeting add to its uniqueness and potential fruitfulness as an applicable approach. Readers can decide for themselves whether and to what extent the results of the dialogue are applicable to them, and in what context. Researchers may also want to cull the results for common themes and broader implications.

That said, it was emphatically evident that the participants in the dialogue and many of those who observed them, were palpably moved by what they witnessed. I will have more to say on this following the presentation of the transcript.

The dialogue framework was similar to, though not an exact replica of, the dialogue forms I have outlined in this book. The reasons for this difference are twofold. First, dialogues such as the one below have been rich learning experiences for me, and I have made modifications based on those experiences. Second, the participants were comparatively more psychologically minded than many other participants I've worked with, which enabled them to engage with comparatively less structure, guidance, and support. Despite such differences, however, I believe the dialogue below is an exemplary demonstration of how the Experiential Democracy Dialogue can proceed and the impact it can have on some of the most critical areas of social life.

The dialogue opens with a background phase, although it was offered more spontaneously rather than solicited. If I facilitated such a dialogue in the present day, I would make a direct request that the parties speak about what it was like to grow up and how the racially other was treated. That said, the parties did touch upon aspects of their youth in this initial phase, which helped to provide context for their subsequent reflections. Following the background phase, we then moved to a turn-taking phase elaborating each one's particular stance toward community policing. This second phase was followed by a more freely flowing discussion about the parties' respective experiences of community policing. Finally, the third phase consisted of the question: What was discovered about yourself and the other through this dialogue, and were there any points of common ground?

Here then is the encounter:

K (Kirk): I'd like to begin with Rodger (the officer) describing—as mindfully and heartfully as possible—your experience of community policing.

R (Rodger): Well my experience goes back a lot of years...really going back to my initial impressions, it was probably the late '80s or early '90s when this issue emerged in the law enforcement community. And I recall that this was our administration's new program. And a lot of us devoted a lot of our time and effort to become trained, and most specifically trained as crime-fighters. Our idea of community policing was quick response and taking quick action to help community victims. But what we got with community policing was going out and socializing with people in the neighborhood. But I remember we had conversations among us that this was really misdirected, again another—what I would say now...bureaucratic patchwork. Just another program so you can say you're making progress. But there was nothing really sold to us about it except this was going to be a way to make neighborhoods safer by involving the public. And by involving the public that initially created anxiety for us because the public doesn't always make the best decisions in emergency situations.

I come from a state where we have open-carry laws. It's a very individualist culture, and the idea of getting a neighborhood involved was like encouraging a partnership with vigilantes—at least that was the potential. So we didn't really want citizens getting involved, since getting citizens involved can get them hurt, and we were the ones who would hurt them.

The other thing is that we had trained so hard and took our jobs so seriously yet now we were expected to go out and meet with neighborhood groups and have lemonade with them. And we thought that this wasn't really a good use of our time. Just to write a traffic ticket takes 20—25 minutes and there's so few resources, and we were often patrolling understaffed, so there were no people out there to give backups sometimes on calls....We really looked at it as if it was a PR thing and not really going to accomplish anything. So I felt resistant to it initially and thought it was a waste of my skills and time, and I thought it was encouraging citizens to get involved in a way that could very easily be counterproductive and wasn't really going to give us what we wanted. But it was ultimately going to make the papers, and it was trying to make the police department look more friendly. And at that period of time...there was a lot of media attention on Rodney King, and so having a nicer, more friendly police department was what the people in the suburbs—whom I worked for—really wanted. And as a night patrol officer....I knew there was a lot going on, and many people knew there was a lot going on, a lot of dangerous stuff. So as a community police officer, [I saw it] as just another program...and like a lot of other programs, [I thought] it would just go away.

It ultimately turned into assignments that people took—officers who were assigned to community work, but those of us on standard patrol rarely heard about them or met with them. We still were out handling radio calls because the calls just kept coming and coming, and that's what you'd do in those days. So I didn't have a lot of faith in community policing...and I didn't have a lot of faith in the people in the neighborhood who were coming to the table. A lot of those people ended up being neighborhood complainers....They were people who complained about every kid in the neighborhood...casing the house.....And particularly with minority kids I can't tell you how many times I got called because a minority kid walked by somebody's house and we had the community-oriented person or community officer contacting the dispatcher saying this is a suspicious person. And then there wasn't much we could do about a kid walking on the sidewalk...so it was a very "rock and a hard place" kind of thing.

K: Okay, thank you. I'm going to cut in at this point and ask Nathaniel if you could feed back to Rodger—again as mindfully as possible—what you heard Rodger expressing.

Nathaniel (N): What I heard from Rodger was that he was put into a position of community policing that he didn't have much faith in at the outset. And part of this community policing—this project—was to include citizens and socializing communities, with the help of citizen involvement. And in theory it sounds [like] it is a great idea.... But I get the sense from you (Rodger) that it was a tool for chaos or that...this was not a good idea because citizens' lives were put in harm's way. And that the idea of socializing communities should be left to law enforcement and not community involvement. And help me understand this because you mentioned minorities and youth.... I get a sense of you having an opinion as to who in the community should be socialized and who should do the socializing. And I have the feeling that the teen who was walking down the street was not part of the process of socializing but that he was targeted, which further added to your anxiety around the whole idea of community policing.

K: Rodger, could you give feedback to Nathaniel as to whether he captured your perspective...reasonably well or is there anything you wanted to add?

R: I think he captured it well. We were committed to equal protection under the law....and we would go into neighborhoods and people would call and say "this is suspicious behavior"...and their idea of suspicious behavior and our idea were not the same...[A]gain, this comes back to the use of resources...we're going out there...to answer someone's anxiety about a minority [kid] walking down the street....What I would say is that there was a particular community that was to be socialized and then there was everybody else. The minority youth was part of that "somebody else" and not the standard suburbanite—what we now say—taxpayer.

K: Okay, Nathaniel would you now take about 5 minutes and describe as mindfully and heartfully as possible your experience of community policing?

N (putting his black hood over his head): When I was in Head Start going into kindergarten, one of the first lessons I learned was that whenever I'd find myself in trouble [I should] look for Officer "Friendly." Officer Friendly was the prototype of my savior, if I could just find Officer Friendly. I had all faith in Officer Friendly. But as time went on on the South Side of Chicago, I grew quickly to fear Officer Friendly. The one who had on the side of his automobile "we're here to protect" became my enemy. And I felt the overwhelming presence of fear whenever I was in the presence of Officer Friendly. That fear continued through my teenage life, and sometimes we'd run just when a police car would come down the street. It wasn't that we were doing anything wrong, that we were breaking any law, but we knew because of our suspicious look...we were guilty before proven innocent. And the result was that the police became part of the establishment—the establishment that I could never be a part of.

Even if I were to get an education, even if I were to transcend the life of the inner-city ghetto, I would still be marked by my suspicious look. Be it the hoodie, be it the dreads, be it the "uniform" that I cannot take off. And it led me to have a sense of fear, a sense of dread that goes far beyond paranoia. Yes, I should be paranoid when I appear in front of a cop, but I shouldn't be so afraid that I pray to God *"Please* don't let me get tased today. *Please* don't let me get shot sixteen times in the back. *Please* don't let something happen today." And that fear gets exacerbated every time I see my sons—young and black like me. I fear for their lives maybe ten times more than I do my own as to what could happen to them in the face of those who "serve to protect."

K: Thank you. Rodger, could you now give feedback to Nathaniel [about] what you heard [him] expressing?

R: Let's start with a characterization, and you can correct me if I'm wrong, but Nathaniel you painted...a picture of innocence—an innocence that you initially trusted—some would say naively—but you had a belief in a character or...a persona that actually worked for you....But over time you lost your faith in that persona and found over time that police officers actually were not friendly and in fact could be quite nasty. And to the point that you became fearful for your personal safety any time that there was...the presence of a police officer. It didn't matter who that police officer was. The uniform that the police officer wears, and takes off every night, represented something menacing to you. And that menacing took on such fear—you call it "healthy fear"— that there's a reasonable and rational amount of caution that you feel. But that you tried not to take it so far that it took you over...but it was still there. Now as a father you're in the role of a protector and your principle role is to protect your black sons from [those] community protectors.

K: Thank you. Now (turning to Nathaniel) do you feel Rodger captured your experience? Or let me put it this way, is there anything you want to add to Rodger's portrait?

N: Absolutely. There's something that stands out from what you said and that is about the uniform, and what that uniform represents. To me the uniform doesn't simply represent the police department. It doesn't simply represent law enforcement. It represents a society that is plagued with systemic racism and degradation. It represents something deeper than "preserve and protect." And that's what scares me. And what really scares me is that your uniform, which represents "menacing," is something that at the end of the day you can take off. But what really scares me is that my uniform [pointing to his skin]—which represents thuggery, menacing, rioting—I can't take it off. And that really freaks me out that my son cannot take off his uniform. And that really scares me.

I remember as a little boy buying "Amby" [a skin lightening product]... so that maybe if I could change the uniform, if I could lighten it up, maybe I would be looked upon as less menacing. Maybe I could be looked upon as not being a thug. [But] to no avail; I could not become light enough. I could not become white enough. I could not become a part of the establishment *enough* even after getting an education. And the first thing that comes to my mind when I'm pulled over by a cop is not that a tail light is missing, not that my tags are missing, or my insurance has run out. The *first* thing that comes to my mind is that I'm a black man being pulled over by a white cop. The first thing is...am I going to live through this situation? And that scares me.

K: Rodger, do you have a response to that statement?

R: I don't know what a bad guy looks like. Early in my career—and I started as a police officer at 21, I'll turn 48 in two weeks—so I've been in law enforcement for 27 years...and I remember an academy instructor telling me that there's two ways you lose your job and that is to be killed or to be politically killed. And if you cross the wrong white person, they'll take your job, but if you cross a black person, they'll take your life. That was 1988, and I thought at that time that the guy was jaded. Now many years later I still remember that guy saying that, and how much he believed it. Perhaps that's what you [Nathaniel] meant when you talked about the establishment. I also remember when we were taught about tattoos. The tattoos meant either that people were in military service or that they were thugs... And in 1988 they were either motorcycle people or they were military people, and it was a good place to start when it came to sorting people out, particularly when you...got to recognize which were jailhouse tattoos. When I was 20 years old, I worked at Utah State prison, and when I was there, I learned behavior and I learned a language and I learned a culture that was not anywhere else. But when I saw it on the street, I learned to identify it very, very quickly—to the point where a friend of mine [who

I worked out with at the gym] when he called me "boss" it would bother me. And I said, "I wish you wouldn't say that," because...I worked in a prison and it puts me in a position where [it creates a division] and puts me on the other side. He later told me he'd done seven years in prison...and so he was a young ex-convict and I was a young officer and he'd served his time.

But what I learned from that is that I don't know what a bad guy looks like. I've dealt with clergy that molested children, which was a huge loss of innocence for me. I saw men beat women that they were supposed to love—unrecognizably, sometimes with weapons. The number of rapes that happened in our city...that nobody ever knew about was amazing. And then there's the traffic encounter...and the one thing you learn about traffic encounters is that you never know who you're stopping....I've stopped menacing white people that were in suits, that turned out to be a bigger problem than anybody wearing their hat backwards or having tattoos. I nearly shot a 17-year-old one night...[who] reached in the dark, and I heard metal in the seatbelt and I thought I was done. So I don't know what bad guys look like...they drive a lot of different cars. The one thing I do know is that the better bad guys learn to blend. The younger bad guys like to wear the bad guy uniforms. The thugs in the neighborhoods like to advertise that they're bad guys. But the real ones that are real dangerous are really into organized crime. And they really don't sweat patrol officers...but their crime is so much worse and so much deeper that it really has nothing to do with neighborhood watch. We're talking about major drug trafficking and stuff like that. So that's what I saw in my own community...so that's what I reflect back to you. I don't know what a bad guy looks like.

N: I hear that but I also hear the words you said you heard early on. That the white legislator will take your job but the *black man will take your life!* And it stands to reason that—even though you don't know what a bad guy looks like—it was instilled in you that you know that the black man will take your life. And that's the bad kind. It's not so much the one who will take your job but it's the one who'll take your life. And my question is that: How does [one] know that won't impact your behavior as a cop?...Does that differentiate your behavior towards one from another?

R: I found...what that academy instructor said... [as an officer working the suburbs] not to be true. In fact, what I found was that it was a lot more the opposite. That stopping a black man for a traffic violation was more likely to generate a complaint with my chief than stopping a white man. And that created a certain amount of anxiety too. Now all of a sudden I didn't know how this was going to go. I didn't know if I was going to walk out and be met with a friendly conversation...and I'll also say this, I think with most citizens a traffic stop is a traumatic event; for me when I see blue and reds in my mirror, I get anxious. And I also know that this young officer who is going to walk up to me is going to ask for my license and registration, and I also know that I have a pistol in my car....and so that changes my conversation with him too. I have to talk to him in a way that communicates "I'm armed but I'm a good guy." But again, police officers don't know who's a good guy or bad guy...so there's some anxiety there. But what I found out is that oftentimes the only encounter the average citizen has with a police officer is a traffic stop...

K: I just wonder how you both feel right now facing each other, hearing each other, in each other's uniforms, so to speak. I wonder what your experience of each other is. Nathaniel, you brought up what a powerful symbol a police uniform is. Rodger, you implied that it is as well...

N: For me there's a perpetual state of confusion when I talk with someone like Rodger here who doesn't fit the cop schema that I have in my mind. And the cop schema I have in my mind says that you don't have my best interests at heart. But then, the times I've had to rely on cops, more often than not, [they] do have my best interests at heart, and so I'm pulled in these different polarities—that "wow, this is a pretty good dude; I should trust him." In fact, I don't want to lean too far away from him just in case something happens in the neighborhood. But then, on the other hand, it just scares the crap out of me that that one bad cop will look at my "uniform" and size me up based on me looking suspicious because I'm different from them. And it's not so much that I'm afraid of the white cop; it's more that I'm afraid of the white cop's fear of me. And because that white cop is afraid of me as a black man, they will do anything to reduce that threat, even if it means taking my life when I pose no threat whatever. So it's not that I'm afraid of you (pointing to Rodger); I'm afraid of your fear towards me.

K: Do you, Rodger, have a reaction to what Nathaniel expressed?

R: ...I understand what Nathaniel is saying and I think it's valid, particularly because we come from very different worlds. The south side of Chicago is very different than where I grew up. In fact, I remember an early lesson. We had a black girl come into our high school and one of the teachers said to the students, "You know, it's really obvious you're going out of your way to befriend this new student, but actually it's an overcompensation," because it was like a celebrity was in town [in that] we had one black student and it was almost paradoxically insulting....But the feeling I have with   the systemic part of it [which I term the "bureaucracy" says]: "Now we have a new police program. We're going to hire more diverse [officers], we're going to recruit more diverse [officers]. All these things are frustrations because these are political solutions to what patrol officers perceive as practical problems. I want to go out and I want to catch bad guys; I want the bad guys in jail, and I don't really care what color they are.

Nathaniel, you and I have talked about this so it's sort of a cheat, but right from the beginning, you've recognized my uniform and I've recognized yours. And we stand there together in a place of gathering that I've been invited into and you've been invited into. We have to work out the uniform thing before we can proceed as human beings...learn more about each other as human beings. It's not something you created and it's not something I created but it's a source of fear; it's a source of frustration. There's a lot of negative emotions that come in with that...

K: You (Rodger) feel a lot of negative emotions?

R: I feel a lot of frustration, and there's a lot of frustration that comes in every single day. Every single...Facebook post and the way social media is nowadays there's a lot of derogatory things posted about police officers. And I've seen YouTube video after YouTube video of a white police officer doing something that shocks my conscience.... But what I hear Nathaniel saying is that [coming from] his healthy fear or...anxiety...[he] recognizes that [shocking] possibility. I recognize that possibility too, and I think those officers ought to go to jail...

The other thing that I know is that because the system is bureaucratic that whether I shoot somebody and it was absolutely necessary or not, there's going to be a period where I'm going to be under trial and I'm going to be considered guilty before proven innocent. I have friends who have been considered guilty before being proven innocent, even though they've been exonerated by the authorities. They lost their jobs politically because it was not popular for the police department to keep them on the job. They have lost other jobs in police departments because that [particular] police department doesn't want [it known] in the media that this officer is working again. Even though they've been exonerated of any wrongdoing.

So there's a lot of frustration that these community programs are...creating a bigger wedge than they're doing anything...

K: Unfortunately, we have limited time, but if we were to go on I might go more deeply into the issue of your whiteness/blackness and how this figures into the mix of community policing. But given our limited time, I'd like to move to the next phase...which is: Do you feel you've come to any sense of common ground or ideas about what could be helpful in regard to community policing from your respective experiences?

N: I do. I'm actually very appreciative of Rodger's admission of what [he] would do to those cops. So what I'm hearing from you is just because they wear the uniform, just because they wear the badge, they're not good. And just because I wear this uniform [he points to his hoodie], it doesn't automatically make me bad. And so I appreciate that; that means a lot to me to hear that...

K: And you feel that as well as hear it?

N: I do feel that. It doesn't ameliorate the fear...and if I can just read this, it only takes about two minutes. [Kirk nods in agreement]. This is a poem that I wrote in reference to community policing.

The title is "What I Fear"[2]:

> Are you so afraid
> Of my skin so brown
> You use all possible means
> To keep me down
>
> Are you so afraid
> You have to lock me up

---

[2] "What I Fear" was originally published in *Stay Awhile: Poetic Narratives on Multiculturalism and Diversity*, by Louis Hoffman & Nathaniel Granger, Jr. (University Professors Press, 2015).

Keep me shackled
Kick my butt

I'm not afraid of you
Let me make that clear
Your baseless fear of me
Is what I fear

Are you so afraid
That I look suspicious
That like a rabid dog
You attack so vicious

Getting autographs
While at the gun show
While your victim marked absent
Another "No Show"

Another Black teen
'Sleep in the mortuary
No remorse, your conscience clean
Evil portuary

I'm not afraid of you
Let me make that clear
Your baseless fear of me
Is what I fear

Are you so afraid
Of the way I talk
You will kill me dead
For the way I walk

Are you so afraid
That I'll take your power
When I simply want to bloom
Like any other flower

By George, I pray
Remove this fear
Before another murder

A mother's graveside tear

I'm not afraid of you
Let me make that clear
Your baseless fear of me
Is what I fear.

K [visibly moved]: Rodger, do you have any more thoughts [or] feelings...about a basis for common ground?

R: Well, I think the common ground and some faith is that...[Nathaniel] says he experiences some confusion, that, on the one hand, everything in that poem is based on experiences, is based on a perspective. [But] for me to hear that poem with the pronoun "you" feels contentious. It's a little difficult for me to hear [Nathaniel] read me that poem, given the relationship we already have. And so I have to take that division that we have and say "okay, this is a poem" and not take it personally.

But it does go to...what I think we share in common, and that is objectification. I feel objectified all of the time when I perform [police duties]. Sometimes people are over-ingratiating [they] wanna buy coffee, want to do all these things, and it's like "you know what I just want to do my job." When 9/11 happened people would come up and say "Thank you so much for your services." And it's all meant well; we just want to do our job. But we're inhibited from doing our job...there's a negative there too. That negativism is perpetuated not by African American activists. It's perpetuated by every police officer that commits crimes against the citizenry. I think the thing that we agree on is that there's nothing worse than a dirty cop....The other thing that I heard from you [Nathaniel], and that I think puts that together, is you said that "every time you've needed an officer an officer had your best interest." So if you've experienced that [then] the negative experiences you have...are protective feelings; they're survival feelings. The good feelings you have are pleasant but they don't really touch you in that survival way—and they don't threaten you. And being threatened is different; it's a different thing, and I feel the exact same way. And...where we come to together is that neither one of us is willing to presume that even though our uniforms are different that we're necessarily on a different side.

K: That feels like a very important issue—the presumption issue [Rodger says "absolutely"], and it would be important to pursue. But because we have limited time, one of the things it makes me think of is whether this kind of process [the experiential democracy dialogue] might be helpful both in the community and with police officers, where it's more of a one-on-one sharing experience. Facilitated hopefully in...an optimally safe setting.

R: I'd like to point something out, and that is that Nathaniel here is representing...a population in the United States. As an individual sitting here, he's the spokesperson for a race...And I'm sitting here as a spokesperson for a very diversified and decentralized occupation. And that puts us in positions of responsibility for actions that we're not responsible for. And for attitudes that we're not responsible for. And for a historical trajectory that neither one of us created. And yet what we're doing is that we're sitting down person-to-person and saying "Okay, world, all of the historical trajectory, all of the establishment and [those who are] unestablished—all that is important stuff to understand but really at some point [Nathaniel] and I have to meet together, and we have to do something about it or the story carries on.

K: We can create the story here...

R: Maybe for us, maybe for some of you [pointing to the audience]. But the other thing that we agree on is that when it comes to street encounters there's a healthy fear on both sides.

Follow-up Questions from the Audience
Member of audience: What kind of [police] training do you think would be most effective?

N: To answer that if I may, I think one of the greatest trainings would be a greater focus on multicultural awareness. I'm not talking about a six-week course and then you get a certificate. But I'm talking about maybe a six-month course or a year course in order to understand the different nuances associated with different cultures. And to understand...behaviors that are unique to different cultures. I know that as an African American male that African American men meet the criteria for anti-social personality disorder. When the fact of the matter is that their behaviors are just a way of survival, and even though their behavior meets the criteria for anti-social personality disorder, they're just trying to survive in the hood. And I think cops—law enforcement—need to understand that.

If you tell me to take my hands out of my pocket and put my hands up...I mean, it's not that I have a weapon, but maybe I just didn't understand, maybe I'm just afraid...whatever. Don't just shoot me because I didn't respond as quickly as you thought I should respond. Because I'm afraid, and when I'm afraid I freeze up. I'm hearing you but my body doesn't want to respond because I'm stuck. And so I think training should emphasize multicultural diversity—and cultural empathy. Like coming out of your uniform and putting on "black face"; [learning] what it's like to be black for a day.

K: Would you reverse that for the black community [to learn what it's like to be a police officer for a day]?
N: Absolutely, I believe there should be an exchange of training, not just for law enforcement but even for the community...[like making] workshops [available].

K: Is that true for you [pointing to R]?

R: I think what Nathaniel said is right on—and I don't know if we've talked about this before—but the frustration that I have is with the bureaucrats. So then the bureaucrats, the policymakers, can then say..."we've done something about this. So the next officer who shoots a black man is completely responsible for all of that," and [the bureaucrats] are going to say, "We've got this multicultural program and we're good....you know, that's not our fault because we provided training."
    ....The system hasn't worked for hundreds of years, and so we've got to figure out how to get people to engage person-to-person....But one of the things we do is talk about the macro-level and policies, and then we do the bureaucrat thing all over again....But if we can get people to do the kind of work that you're doing [referring to K and the present dialogue] at the local level, [then] deal with your community, deal with your cops. If you want your children to be safe you have to go to your local police department and say, "What can I do to help?" And then expect that healthy fear.

Discussion
The foregoing dialogue is one of the rare moments when an African American activist and a White police officer shared intimate experiences both of each other and the communities they represent. Yet encounters such as these don't need to be rare. In fact, they should

become frequent, if not commonplace. It seems clear to me, as it was to the two dialogue partners, that meetings such as the one they underwent are integral if both community members and law enforcers are going to get at the root of their frustrations with one another, and if they're to dispel stereotyping, as well as the cycle of polarization. As both Nathaniel and Rodger recognized, the way to stand even a chance of mending differences is not generally through fortifying them, but facing them, trying to understand them, and trying to build a basis on which trust and friendship can deepen.

At the very least, and as both Nathaniel and Rodger reaffirmed with me following the meeting, the Experiential Democracy Dialogue or a variant of it should be tried by both community members and the police. It might make sense to start with a few select facilitators, officers, and citizens from a local community as a pilot project. The outcome of the project could then be analyzed for its difficulties and successes, and as a working basis for follow-up meetings. These meetings in turn could continue the process of refining and broadening the scope of the project, so that, potentially, sizeable regions of the country can find new ways to coexist, if not bond.

That said, there are, of course, many elements of the above dialogue that could and should, in my view, be reflected on. These elements have implications for addressing fear, racism, presumption, suspicion, enmity, shame, desperation, alienation, and many other aspects. But perhaps equally striking is the dialogue's illumination of tolerance, humaneness, authenticity, empathy, connection, and possibly even love at some level. Nathaniel's poem was painful for Rodger (and all to whom it was addressed), but it was equally a cry for validation, aspiration, and humanization, which Rodger also seemed to recognize. By the same token, Rodger's acknowledgment of his own reactivity, sense of being objectified, and sense of being grossly misunderstood at times was difficult for Nathaniel, but at the same time it seemed quite clear that he found Rodger's lament relatable, valid, and worthy of acknowledgment. These then are the seedlings of a transformation, both internally and between the parties. They are the bellwethers for communal and institutional reassessment, reengagement, and reform.

In sum, what seemed most helpful to the dialogue partners is that they were supported to be civil with each other; that they had more facets to their points of view than they originally perceived; and strikingly, that they both desired what each side expressed. These desires included government support for necessities: city services, law and order, and justice. Moreover, they included people's right to protect their families and neighborhoods, human decency, and the sense that *balance* is key. This was especially notable when it came to issues such as self vs. societal interests, safety vs. coercion, practicality vs. legalities, freedoms of expression vs. social order. The fact that these issues were perceived as lying along a continuum rather than as categorical absolutes was hopeful for the dialogue partners.   It meant that negotiation, the potential for a "win–win" alternative, was not only possible but evident and within reach.

Finally, although it wasn't overt, I sensed that Nathaniel and Rodger experienced hints of awe in their communications. As trying as their dialogue became at times, they also approached each other with curiosity and earnest efforts to learn about each other. I deeply felt that they bracketed many assumptions about each other and approached their encounter with a sense of mystery and adventure that was far from comfortable, but that engaged them. They were engaged with meeting each other—really meeting, venturing, and seeing what might emerge from the entire process.

Three Years Later
Three years after the above Experiential Democracy Dialogue, I invited Nathaniel Granger and Rodger Broome to reflect on their experiences and share their insights about what, if anything, they have discovered over the ensuing years. Below are their testimonies—incisive, candid, and heartfelt.

Nathaniel Granger's Reflection on the Dialogue
It is important as a (so-called) minority, to know that those in positions of power, specifically law enforcement, understand me as a person before handling my personage to any degree. When understanding is lacking, however, it is likely that my behaviors, as well as the behaviors of those in power, become absolutist, rooted in fear of "other." Moreover, systems and those operating within those systems become tyrannical, alienating the "other." This rigidity leads to fragmentation resulting from already experienced and/or perceived trauma. In order to cope, dissociation occurs, and traumatic experiences are compartmentalized in the brain so as to keep one from feeling too much pain, be it physical, emotional, or both. When racism is the substratum upon which any action is implemented, the lines of understanding are blurred and the divide exacerbated, as with the current state of the relationship between the Black citizen and the White cop. In his 2016 book, *The Table of Brotherhood: How to View and Discuss Racial*

Disparities, Injustices and Party Politics Across the Racial and Political Divide, Mathis posited:

> With the current racial divide widening in America [and] with every racial incident our nation is in need of healing and true reconciliation. In a section from Martin Luther King Jr's "I have a Dream" speech we can find a vital key necessary to make this a reality – Sitting down at the Table of Brotherhood. In this section of the speech we can see the canvas of the racial backdrop of the two distinct histories in America...those of African descent and those of European descent – the sons of former slaves and the sons of former slave owners. This canvas shows us the lens through which each group's vision of life was formed and focused, and why we see the way we see and think the way we think on each side of the racial divide. (pp. 10–11)

The Table of Brotherhood about which King spoke and Mathis expounded was one where opposing parties, such as Blacks and Whites, could come together in a safe place to discuss opposing views. Similarly, the "Experiential Democracy Dialogue" is a forum where two people representing diverse backgrounds and/or ethnicities are asked to engage in a phase model that supports personal, one-on-one conversation. The purpose of the Experiential Democracy Dialogue, conceived by Kirk Schneider "as a way to enlarge and deepen the democratic process of deliberation," is to provide a comparatively safe, facilitated space where participants of different backgrounds can share each other's stories, express each other's social–political concerns, and potentially find a "bridge" or "meeting ground" on which understanding and support may be built. Its intent is to foster dialogue between individuals from different walks of life and opposing views and, in the case in which I was involved, to provide an example to both communities and law enforcement about the deeper element of democracy, which is facing each other as human beings.

As shown in the above transcript, Rodger, a White police officer, and I, a Black man, faced one another, toe-to-toe, to discuss the implications of race on policing. What I understood from Rodger was that the police were called into neighborhoods to deal with "suspicious behavior," not realizing that their idea of suspicious behavior was not suspicious to the ones targeted. Despite the idea that community policing's goal is to socialize communities with a collaborative effort of utilizing community members and police to socialize the community, when it comes to minorities, the premise is that although the goal is for everyone to work together, the minority who is expected to work collaboratively with law enforcement is the same minority who in the eyes of a microaggressive system, needs to be socialized. With Kirk Schneider facilitating, Rodger and I were able to establish a bridge with which to discuss our respective views—a bridge with which communication was fostered and shared as opposed to hurled at one another. Through a series of steps, it was demonstrated how the experiential process can proceed. During the illustration, we both had to see each other as who we were, apart from the given context— Rodger as Rodger and me as me, each in our raw form. As the demonstration advanced, I saw in front of me a White cop and was certain that Roger saw me as a Black activist. In a naturalistic environment, it was apparent that the two of us would not have been able to engage in healthy dialogue based on our divergent views. However, through the Experiential Democracy Dialogue, we were able to empathize with one another. For me, this took the form of seeing the victimization of a White police officer by a system that conditioned him to see behaviors more readily than people. Furthermore, we were both able to humanize one another. For example, we humanized each other enough to realize that we both wanted to survive; that we both had fears, and that we both were part of a system that has perpetually kept us divided.

Ultimately, and again, we could see each other's humanness through this encounter, resulting in a more proactive engagement as opposed to one that was essentially reactive. These apparently powerful results can promote similar dialogues both in communities and governments.

Rodger Broome's Reflection on the Dialogue
The encounter that I shared with Drs. Schneider and Granger was a potent one. When we initially discussed doing it, I proposed that I wear my uniform so that I would be stigmatized by those who might be wary of police. Activists express concerns about the unconscious biases of police officers against racialized minorities (especially males), but there is also a counter-stigmatization against police uniforms by anti-police activists. So much floating around on the internet are legitimate human emotions wrapped up in hyperbole to group people into categories and leverage them for political agendas. Polarization is salient in our society like I have never seen before in my life.

The most surprising thing about our encounter was the felt sense of realness for me. It helped me to believe in the possibilities of Schneider's mode of healing. Dr. Granger and I have been friends for around 5 years, and I was concerned that the encounter at the conference would be tainted by that fact, and the fact that we both have advanced education. But once we got into our places and engaged, the emotions and thoughts were authentic. I felt very much like a police officer giving an account for my brothers and sisters in blue, and for all of the viral videos and sensationalized news stories presented to the world. At one point, Dr. Granger read a poem with a hoodie sweatshirt pulled up (signifying Trayvon Martin) and, the psychodrama in contradistinction to my police uniform was powerful. We still had a lot left to say when our time ran out. I am pleased that Schneider is now moving forward with a book that includes the encounter. It was not play-acting or merely a drill. For me, this was a high-stake dialog that I hope others can learn from without filtering it through a theoretical lens. We met as human beings that would seemingly fall on opposite sides of an issue, but we agree that peace and justice are the goals.

A Therapeutic Application
of the Experiential Democracy Dialogue

What follows is an inner journey utilizing principles of existential therapy to facilitate an Experiential Democracy Dialogue. This approach, which was remarkably rich, both for myself and my partner in the journey, Serge Prengel, should be applied in safe and supportive settings such as a therapist's office or between capable colleagues. In fact, I would strongly advise those utilizing this approach to have a basic background in depth psychological approaches such as existential–humanistic or psychodynamic therapies, and in the case of at least one of the partners, to be (or have been) a licensed mental health practitioner. The reason for these parameters is that the approach entails subtle capacities to work with personally charged emotions for a concerted period of time (such as an hour). The approach also requires a facilitator schooled in the art of creating an alliance, forming an empathic relationship, and cultivating personal and interpersonal presence.

With these ingredients permeating, the following case example of this intimate experiential democracy dialogue proceeded spontaneously. The dialogue began as an intriguing podcast interview arranged by the somatic therapist Serge Prengel concerning my concept of the polarized mind. The "interview," however, quickly transformed into an intimate journey, in which Serge became the interviewee and I the facilitator. The result struck Serge and me as a potentially fruitful edge in the intensification and deepening of conflict mediation—if not the substrata of the democratic process itself—a substrata, by the way, that evokes the awe and wonder of life.

Hence, through Serge's eloquent reflection below, we offer the interview here.   Again, please note that this illustration is but a beginning. It is one possible route toward inner exploration and inner healing in the context of social or cultural conflict. The degree to which that exploration and inner healing succeeded is left to the reader, but Serge and I certainly felt heartened by the experience. Finally, it cannot be overstated that to the degree that people can find the capacity for inner coexistence, their capacity for outer coexistence (in the relational world) is a far likelier prospect.

Here then is Serge's eloquent meditation on our encounter, highlighting the various implications of what we shared together (e.g., "relational implicit"), what we experienced personally (e.g., "somatic implicit"), and what we shared in the context of the culture (e.g., "collective implicit") out of which we emerged.

Going Deep:
An Intimate Excursion into the Polarized Mind
By Serge Prengel

What happens when we get polarized? How can we avoid polarization to engage in more enriching discussions? In this section, I would like to share some thoughts based on an experiential exploration of polarization.

The experience I am drawing upon was not a polarized discussion. It was a collaborative endeavor in which I remembered experiences of polarization to better understand them. I will be bringing up a contrast between this collaborative atmosphere and the circumstances under which we get more polarized.

The Initial Shift
The conversation started as an interview. The roles were clear. I was the interviewer, and Kirk Schneider was the person interviewed. We were going to talk about a topic he has thought about a lot and written a book about: *The Polarized Mind*. We didn't go very far with the

conventional interview portion. Soon after the beginning, we shifted the format of the conversation.

It started with my suggestion that we proceed carefully: We were not discussing a neutral topic, but one which could emotionally touch our audience. I disclosed that I could, at times, have a polarized mind. Kirk suggested that we explore the topic experientially. Effectively, we shifted roles, with him leading me through a process of experiential exploration. Before we went any further into this process, we established some rules for safety. All of this evolved organically.

When an interview takes place, some things are so evident that it is not necessary to state them explicitly. There are specific roles: the interviewer and the interviewee. The manner of the interview may vary, but both parties share the implicit assumptions. They constitute a stable framework for the interchange—I think about it as the Shared Implicit.

Through a process of attunement, we restructured our Shared Implicit. It involved paying attention to implicit clues and resulted in making the space safe and comfortable much faster than a ponderous explicit negotiation might have. As a result, we broadened the field of the possible. This early step set the tone for the possibility of further expansion during the rest of the conversation.

Embodied Experience

An experiential exploration means paying attention to the experience from inside, as opposed to talking about it as if it were outside. Exploring inner experience involves paying attention to body sensations.

In this case, we were not in the midst of a polarized discussion. Still, I was recollecting polarized interactions to access my inner experience of them. Here is what came up for me. I noticed the tightening of my shoulders, a shallower breath, a sense of my spine folding in—all of this subtle, not necessarily visible to an outside observer.

These physical sensations were not random. They were the result of my whole organism reacting to the situation. They were "bottom-up" implicit reactions, as opposed to "top-down." Through neuroscience findings, we are keenly aware that much of our functioning is at a "bottom-up," implicit level. Somatic mindfulness involves being in touch with embodied experience—i.e., the Somatic Implicit.

As we stay present with our experience, a felt sense forms, which is the way we experience the Somatic Implicit. In this case, my felt sense of the experience comes down to a simple handle: a sense of rigidity.

Conversely, as I shifted to the opposite of the polarized mind, the experience was a sense of fluidity.

Interestingly, Kirk had defined the polarized mind as a "fixation on a single point of view to the utter exclusion of competing points of view." The bodily sense of rigidity, the opposite of fluidity, made this concept come to life. It was not an abstract idea, but a felt experience of the Somatic Implicit.

Tracking the Somatic Implicit

Another bodily experience I had during this exploration was a sense of energy in my feet. It felt like they wanted to move. At the time, the meaning I associated with this experience was that it was a "flight" response.

The purpose of the exploration we were conducting was not to dive deep into the embodied experience, so we left it at that. Now, having had more time to revisit the experience, I have a somewhat different sense of it. I now think of it as something similar to what happens in the Wile E. Coyote cartoons. When he walks past the edge of the cliff and realizes he's no longer on firm ground, his feet are frantically moving as if to try to generate a firm ground. We can see the panic on his face as he's trying to prevent the inevitable fall into the abyss.

There is a commonality to the earlier sense I had of this experience and the one that came up after staying with it longer. In both cases, it was a sense of fear. The image of Wile E. Coyote gives it further dimension. It is a sense of losing ground. What happens then? A sense of being in free fall, a terrifying existential fear.

Conversely, later in the conversation, there came the point where I felt that the energy was no longer just in my feet. I could feel it moving throughout my body, including my torso. I experienced a sense of fluidity. In hindsight, as I revisit the experience, I can see that the earlier experience of energy in the feet alone corresponded to a disconnection from my upper body. Of course, this is very consistent with fear.

What is it that made it possible to dissipate the fear? As we continued the conversation, as I felt further supported by the connection achieved through the Shared Implicit and the increased connection to my body, I became more grounded. I believe that this enabled me to have a more integrated experience of my body and experience energy as fluidity.

Becoming aware of the Somatic Implicit and the supportive Shared Implicit helped move me from defending to exploring. It is good to know that there is a way to do so. However, the question remains: What is it that can cause such intense reactions in the first place?

The Somatic Implicit is the bottom-up reaction of the organism to the situation (or to the perceived situation). So, what was the felt meaning of what I experienced? It felt like the sudden loss of something that was anchoring me. It happened as I was paying attention to situations in which discussions get polarized, with topics such as politics, economics, social issues, religious issues.

The Power of Myth

What these topics have in common is that they are about myths, in the sense that historian Yuval Harari assigns to myth in his book, *Sapiens*. For him, myth is not a derogatory term, implying fraud or delusion; far from it. Myths are the glue that binds societies together, small tribes as well as countries or supranational entities.

We are accustomed to thinking in these terms when we talk about primitive societies, held together by their religious myths. But, for Yuval Harari, this is not limited to the religious or spiritual realm. Myths are not the exclusive property of primitive societies. The more complex the culture, the more deeply rooted the myths.

In Yuval Harari's framework, money is a myth. It does not have an intrinsic value, and it gets its value by the trust that people have in it. A dollar bill is a worthless piece of paper unless there are people that believe in it enough to give you substantial goods in exchange for it.

Business entities, big and small, are myths. Just like the gods of yore, they are imaginary entities. What is it that makes people believe in Apple enough to make it worth almost a trillion dollars? We trust that the people who make up this company have found some secret sauce that will keep getting consumers to happily part with their money.

In describing the pillars of society as myths, Yuval Harari is not saying that they are illusions that we should eliminate. Quite the contrary. His point is that human cultures simply could not function without these myths. This is why I prefer to refer to these constructs as our Collective Implicit, rather than myths.

In other words, our society (like all societies) rests on a consensus around some foundational myths. It could not function without this consensus. So, what would happen if we were to lose this common ground? It would feel as if we no longer had a ground to stand on. Freefall. Something similar to the fear I described above.

Experiential Exploration of Polarization
I am now coming back to the conversation with Kirk.

At times, I experienced a sense of calm when contemplating the possibility of opposite views. This calm was an embodied experience of equanimity, as opposed to polarization. There is an important caveat. I felt this sense of calm when dealing with the theoretical consideration that views opposite to mine could be valid. But I felt more inner turmoil as soon as I started considering some specific issues (e.g., climate change, impeachment). My experience would then go back to something like the sense of losing ground that I have described before. As I now listen to the recording of our conversation, I can hear the stress in my strained voice and a more disjointed sentence structure.

There is a big difference between valuing equanimity and experiencing it when faced with an issue that is important to you. During the conversation, I mentioned the contrast between my values (to be open to other people and points of view) and my experience (feeling compelled to hold onto a position). The threatening experience was not that of somebody attacking me. Neither was it precisely that of the ground falling from under my feet. It was more a sense of not having something substantial to hang onto.

I will try here to translate this embodied experience into conceptual terms. When dealing with an issue that is important to me, such as climate change, having a polarized view gives me a sense of clarity that grounds me. I perceive two starkly different sides to the issue: One is "reality" and what it implies in terms of which actions to take. The other is a refusal to face reality and making a terrible situation worse. The stakes are high, so there is no margin for error. I hang onto the "right" side.

Evolutionarily, there has been a great value to this kind of clarity. When faced with a clear and present danger, it served our remote ancestors to narrow their focus and marshal all their resources to deal with the threat. Occasional false alarms were a small price to pay for the survival value of reactivity.

Back to current times: What happens when I hang onto this kind of clarity in a polarized discussion? I experience a sense of rigidity and narrowness. It is counterproductive. The situation calls for relying on my mindful brain to develop convincing arguments and mobilizing my social engagement skills to establish a connection with others.

How to Counter Reactivity

Reactivity is counterproductive. We have to develop countervailing skills to go around it or, as the Buddhists say, "skillful means." To effectively do so, we need to embrace the reality that reactivity is ingrained in us, and we cannot will it to disappear. Fortunately, we can regulate the fears that cause reactivity.

We can do so by reinforcing the experience of connection. By sensing the quality of the relationship that we have with each other (the Shared Implicit), we can choose to enhance it consciously. As we do this, we create a moment-by-moment experience of connection and grounding that counters the experience of unraveling.

Being mindful of our felt experience (the Somatic Implicit) helps us broaden our perspective. As we track our physical sensations and our felt sense of the situation, we become less hyperfocused on the ideas we are discussing.

To use a metaphor: If we see awareness as some sort of a container of experience, this container has now become a larger container. It does not just contain the topic; it also includes the sense that I am a human being who is involved in a discussion about a given topic.

In paying attention to our inner experience, we increase peripheral awareness. This awareness makes us more likely to be aware of what is happening between us (the Shared Implicit). It also helps us be more conscious of the mythical nature of what we consider to be self-evident truths (the Collective Implicit).

The Virtuous Cycle

What happens then is the opposite of a vicious cycle: Somatic mindfulness reduces nervous system activation and facilitates access to the more mindful circuits of our brain.

As a result, our capacity for peripheral awareness increases. We become more able to engage with what is between us (Shared Implicit). Thus, we are better able to navigate the intricacies of interaction. It is not that it gives us total control, but it helps us have more ability to influence the dance of cooperation. For instance, we can take intentional steps to make the interaction less adversarial, more collaborative.

Broader peripheral awareness also helps us be more aware of the context (Collective Implicit). As we are less caught up in a cycle of threat and defensiveness, we are more able to remember that we are not dealing with absolute truths, but with myths. With this awareness in mind, we have options to redirect the focus of our conversation. For instance, we might look for where we might have some myths in common and pay attention to what unites us as opposed to just what separates us.

Embracing the Myth of Democracy

The logic of myth is different from the logic of objective reality. A physical phenomenon exists regardless of what you think of it. A myth, such as money, exists only to the extent that people act on their belief in it. To make democracy work, we need to believe in it and act on this belief.

What does it mean in terms of having productive conversations?

- We take it for granted that we simply cannot find an answer that is going to end the argument objectively. In other words, we become aware of the Collective Implicit.
- We shift our goal, from arguing to exploring. In other words, we notice the Shared Implicit and restructure it. This idea is consistent with Kirk's experience in facilitating dialogue between people of different belief systems through the Braver Angels process. Fostering civility in the dialogue helps support the shift to mutual acceptance.
- We stay mindful by tracking our sensations and felt sense. We also take into consideration the other person's experience by paying attention to their tone of voice and body language. Awareness of the Somatic Implicit broadens our sense of the interaction: It is not just an interaction of ideas, but human beings. Feeling this way deepens our capacity for empathy.
- We are now able to have a multilevel conversation. We focus on the level of enrichment that comes from paying attention to the various aspects of the Relational Implicit. As we let go of resolving the issue in a narrow sense, we use the discussion to expand our awareness of the many layers that are part of this issue for each of us. Out of this new awareness, it may even be possible for a new consensus to emerge, something different from the two poles that previously seemed to limit the field.[3]

---

[3] Note: The above passage was drawn from an article originally titled "Polarized Mind and the Relational Implicit." For the full article and interview on which the above was based, see Serge Prengel's website: https://relationalimplicit.com/schneider/

The Experiential Democracy Dialogue
for Politicians and Diplomats

As it is all too obvious to see, our legislative process is broken. The idea of "voting one's conscience," a core of the democratic spirit of deliberation, has too often given way to voting to stay elected, or to appease vested interests, or to attain the "quick-fix"—and the results are petrifying.

As a psychologist schooled in interpersonal mediation, it was this recognition that spurred me to embark on an ambitious project about a dozen years ago: to translate and apply the awe-based principles of presence, freedom, courage, and appreciation to the legislative arena. The core idea of this particular application of the Experiential Democracy Dialogue was to supplement the bureaucratically heavy legislative system with a personal component that would, in theory, provide a counterbalance to what is now a very one-sided, and too often one-dimensional process.

Hence, this proposal below is an adapted version of my original proposal a dozen years ago, and as I watch the inflammatory rhetoric being slung from politicians to spokespeople in the media, I am even more convinced of the proposal's urgency today.

The proposal: A pilot study to consider the efficacy of the "experiential democracy" process—a facilitated one-on-one dialogue between a legislator or diplomat and another (equivalent) party with a contrasting point of view regarding an issue of moral import. The likely benefit of the dialogue is increased ability to tolerate different points of view, increased ability to learn from and understand others' points of view, and increased ability to achieve clearer communication as well as potential for consensus between conflicting parties.

The plan then is to bring together two or more legislators or diplomats representing conflicting views in a safe and confidential setting. A pilot study could then comprise the following steps, which follow the same basic pattern as those we discussed for the Professionally Facilitated Experiential Democracy Dialogue, namely:

1) A trained moderator would facilitate the dialogue and propose that it take place once per week for one hour over a two-week period. (Note that this recommendation is revisable depending on circumstances. If there is a luxury of time, it may be optimal for the dialogue to take place once a week over a four-week period; or if urgent and agreed upon, the dialogue could take

place just once, or several times within a few days. The issue would ultimately need to be decided by the parties involved).

2) The moderator would pledge to the best of their ability that no part of the first four phases of the dialogue—that is, the *Background, Turn-taking, Stereotype/Misportrayal,* and *Question Phases*—will be recorded.

3) The moderator would further pledge that the meeting can occur at a setting of the legislators/diplomats' choosing; and that the first four phases of the meeting would only include the moderator and the two participating legislators/diplomats engaged in the dialogue.

4) The moderator would then recommend that the fifth and final *Discovery/Common Ground Phase* of the dialogue—which comprises the findings or discoveries of the respective participants, along with any potential for consensus on the concerns expressed—be recorded by a person of the legislators' or diplomats' choosing. That person, moreover, would only be invited into the dialogue setting at the start of the fifth phase. This makes sense from both a practical and political perspective. From a practical perspective, it is a lot simpler to collect data pertaining to the outcome of a dialogue than to gather the wealth of details leading up to that outcome; and from a political perspective it is a lot more appealing—if not freeing—for a legislator to engage in a genuine encounter about the details of their personal life as well as political stance without the burden of public scrutiny. Furthermore, the main issues for the constituents of that legislator/diplomat are whether they achieved a capacity to understand and work with the conflicting party, as well as a plan or approach toward how they could work out an accord. Of course, the dialogue partners could decide that one or all of the first four phases be recorded along with the last; this would require the express written consent of *both* the dialogue partners.

5) The final recorded dialogue phase would then be transmitted to either the legislative committee (or leader) responsible for a hearing on that particular topic or to a broader public as determined by the legislative body (committee). The dialogue then becomes part of the official record of that body and represents a new and as yet unprecedented contribution to the legislative process. This is a process that would now be bolstered by a deep, deliberative engagement worthy of a

complex or difficult legislative concern. In effect, then, the Experiential Democracy Dialogue becomes a supplement to the normative deliberations of a legislature. For example, if our country were deciding whether to go to war with a challenging adversary (and had time to do so), it would likely be highly reassuring to the populous if the leader(s) of that decision-making process augmented their deliberations with a representative from the opposing side. Such an Experiential Democracy Dialogue could, in fact, become an indispensable part of the conscience of any substantive deliberative process and thus a normative expansion of our democratic way of life. In any case, these aspirational approaches to our deliberative process can be studied carefully at a later time. What we need now, however, is for some courageous legislators or diplomats to step up and try out the Experiential Democracy process; and we need a legislative body—or even a portion of that body—to support it.

6) The moderator finally would agree to be available for consultation or referral as appropriate if requested by either of the parties to the dialogue.

Suggested Readings and Resources

Buber, M. (1955). *Between man and man* (R.G. Smith, Trans.). Beacon.

Hoffman, L., Cleare-Hoffman, H., Granger, N., & St. John, D. (Eds.). (2020). *Humanistic approaches to multiculturalism and diversity: Perspectives on dxistence and difference.* Routledge.

Mathis, B. T. (2016) *The table of brotherhood: How to view and discuss racial disparities, injustices and party politics across the racial and political divide.* Yeshua Life Publishing.

Prengel, S. (2020, February). Polarized mind and relational implicit. *Relational Implicit.* Retrieved from https://relationalimplicit.com/polarized-mind/.

Rogers, C. (1986). The Rust Workshop: A personal overview. *Journal of Humanistic Psychology.* Retrieved from https://journals.sagepub.com/doi/10.1177/0022167886263003.

Schneider, K. (2016, March). The experiential democracy project: A depth approach to the legislative process. *Mad in America.* Retrieved from https://www.madinamerica.com/2016/03/experiential-democracy/.

Schneider, K., Granger, N., & Broome, R. (2016). Experiential Democracy Project: An I–Thou Dialogue on Community Policing. Retrieved from https://www.youtube.com/watch?v=g92cNF5-Tpw.

Schneider, K., & Krug, O. (2017). *Existential–humanistic therapy* (2nd ed.). American Psychological Association Press.

West, C. (2017). *Race matters.* Beacon Press.

Chapter 5

The Braver Angels Approach:
A Thumbnail Sketch

This is about other people's humanity... You just go through the world looking at it differently... I might not be able to accept somebody's perspective, but I accept them as a person... It isn't worth it to alienate somebody because of their perspectives.
~ Braver Angels workshop participant (Larson, 2020, p.8).

Among the organizations facilitating depolarizing dialogues these days Braver Angels is at the fore. As indicated earlier, Braver Angels (associated with the appeal to the braver and "better angels of our nature" by Abraham Lincoln just prior to the Civil War) is a grassroots movement that emphasizes group dialogues in highly structured, intensively guided formats. The basic impetus for Braver Angels is to "depolarize America" through the cultivation of "curiosity, respect, and openness" between conservative ("Reds" or Republicans) and liberal ("Blues" or Democrats). To this extent the humility and wonder, or sense of adventure toward living, would seem as integral to the Braver Angels' vision, as it is to their programs.

The underlying philosophy of Braver Angels is that by learning about and understanding the positions of others, people will gradually begin to see the common humanity they share, and on that basis bolster the ability to coexist and potentially even thrive with one another. Braver Angels is further predicated on the observation that despite the demonizing sensationalism of our profit-driven world, many people share a desire to be friendly with one another, get to know one another, and find ways to live with one another. The problem, as Braver Angels sees it, is that there are few—if any—spaces to support this underlying desire among people, and even fewer movements that foster it en masse.

With that motivation in mind, Braver Angels provides a series of group formats that promote the skills, structure, and leadership that can mend divides. I know this personally because I've been a workshop moderator for the organization for the past year and a half and have witnessed its transformative power first hand. That said, the organization, like all such movements, has its shortcomings, as I've said earlier, and is learning from its mistakes.

Still, the organization has done a remarkable job with few resources and an all-volunteer membership.[1] Hence, for those willing and able, Braver Angels could be an excellent step toward helping us, as a nation and world, to depolarize. In the spirit of this mission, then, here is a brief sketch—a "roadmap" if you will—of what Braver Angels can offer.

First, I highly recommend that you read about Braver Angels at their website, which can be accessed at www.braverangels.org. This site provides comprehensive information about Braver Angels' mission and services, as well as media coverage and latest news. You will also be highly encouraged to pay the nominal membership fee if you plan to initiate or join in Braver Angels' programs.

As for Braver Angels' services, there are four basic group formats that one can join or initiate (if a format does not exist in one's particular locale). The first format is called an Alliance group. The Alliance group comprises members of a given community who come together to plan, organize, and facilitate "Red–Blue" workshops. The Alliance group, like all Braver Angels groups, is obliged to adhere to Braver Angels' mission and ground rules but has the flexibility to go beyond the planning and organizing of workshops; it can also engage in dialogues about timely issues. Although these dialogues don't generally go into the depth and

---

[1] Braver Angels recently published the results of a survey of post-workshop satisfaction among 1800 plus workshop participants (https://braverangels.org/%20evaluation/), and the results were both consistent and highly favorable. Here's a summary of the results for the Red/Blue workshops:

   1. About 79 percent of participants report that as a result of the experience they are better able to "understand the experiences, feelings, and beliefs of those on the other side of the political spectrum," and more than 70 percent say that they feel more "understood by those on the other side of the political divide."

   2. About three of every four participants report that as a result of the experience they feel "less estranged or angry" with those on the other side, and about the same proportion say that the experience caused them to "learn something that might be helpful to the nation."

intensity of workshop formats, they can still be highly informative and growthful, as I described earlier in this book. Generally, the Alliance dialogues take the form of questions, such as "Why is your view on "x" good for the country?" Or "What platforms do you least like about your political affiliation?" Each person then takes a turn to answer the question without interruption, and sometimes listeners will paraphrase what each speaker says.

A second group format is called a "Skills group." The Skills group is an introductory seminar with heavy emphasis on experiential practice of active listening skills. The Skills group is led by a Braver Angels moderator. All Braver Angels moderators must have a background in group facilitation, are discerningly selected by Braver Angels staff, and are obliged to read through and study hours of Braver Angels materials. These materials consist of pages of guidelines for conducting groups and hours of video presentations of each of the group formats. The final stage of the application process to become a moderator is a group meeting and assessment by Braver Angels staff.

A third group format is called a "Debate group." The Debate group does not involve a political debate, where speakers attempt to "win" for their side. Rather, it "is a highly structured conversation in which a group of people think together, listen carefully to one another, and allow themselves to be touched and perhaps changed by each other's ideas." When done well, this format helps participants move toward a broader and deeper truth and see the validity of diverse views. It also helps to build community relationships. The debate usually consists of 20 or more participants, each of whom must address the Chair of the meeting to reduce direct challenges or grandstanding. The idea is not to present an "air-tight" case, but to articulate what one genuinely believes, no matter how complicated or incomplete. This way people are encouraged to learn about each other as persons and not representatives of a canned point of view.

The fourth and most foundational Braver Angels group format is the "Red–Blue" workshops. As of this writing, there are two such workshops, a three-hour and a six-hour workshop. Each workshop is led by a moderator, is carefully structured, and is optimized for both safety and openness among participants. Generally, there are about five Reds and five Blues at these workshops. All are gathered around a large table in a comfortable setting selected by the organizers of the workshop.

The three-hour workshop consists of four basic segments: An introduction, the facilitation of a stereotypes exercise (summarized earlier in this book); the facilitation of a "fishbowl" in which the respective sides answer pre-set questions such as "How is your political stance good for the country, and what reservations do you hold about your political view?" Following this exercise, the moderator or co-moderators facilitate a concluding dialogue concerning what each respective side has learned about the other, and whether, if at all, there was an attainment of common ground. The six-hour group follows the same basic format as the above but adds more time to explore questions in depth.

To get a flavor of how these groups proceed, here are some notes taken from several groups' engagement of a Questions exercise. These notes reveal the kind of topics participants are concerned about without revealing the identities of the participants, which are strictly confidential.

Here, for example, is how Red (conservative) participants in several workshops formulated questions for their Blue (liberal) counterparts:

1) How does a society measure fairness?
2) With regard to immigration, what are the parameters of asylum, and who should decide?
3) How does a government hold itself accountable in a state dominated by one party?
4) How do you expect and want to pay for universal healthcare?
5) What does border security look like?
6) At what point do we start back to work in the face of the coronavirus?

Now here is a composite of questions formulated by Blues for Red groups:

1) Does President Trump align with your conservative values? And in what ways does he fail to align with those values?
2) Do Republicans believe in healthcare as a universal right?
3) How do your conservative values align with the current executive (presidential) balance of power and how it is implemented?
4) Is there a time when conservatives object to the Administration's actions?
5) What can be done when the individual or community is not able or willing to help those in need?

6) How do you feel about the government's response to the needs for mass testing and contact tracing prior to return to work orders?

In addition to these group formats, there is a "one-on-one" format that has recently been developed called "Conversations Across the Political Divide (CAPD)." [2] This format shares similarities with the "Experiential Democracy Dialogue for Everyday People (EDDEP)" but with several notable distinctions: The CAPD format assumes that at least one of the dialogue partners has participated in a Braver Angels workshop, either online or in person before engaging in the CAPD approach, whereas the EDDEP has no such requirement, although the capacity for civility is assumed. That said, it is important to note that participation in a Braver Angels workshop *could be* a useful supplement regardless of the type of dialogue format chosen. Second, the CAPD approach is focused strictly on political (red/blue) issues, whereas the EDDEP can entail dialogues about broader social issues—whether cultural, religious, or political. Third, the sequence and content of the respective formats are somewhat different, with the CAPD stressing less about "inner" preparation (e.g., experiential visualization of the other party, habituation to emotions and body sensations associated with engaging with the other party) than the EDDEP format. Fourth, upbringing and family influences are also not as directly pursued by the CADP format relative to the EDDEP format. For a fuller comparison of the respective formats visit the section on CAPD at the Braver Angels website noted above.

To sum, I highly recommend participation in Braver Angels workshops and programs. They are trailblazing and provide an enormous opportunity to depolarize minds. They are accessible and widespread, and they are profoundly moving, at least for many. Personally, I have been deeply impressed by the humanity of these groups, their promotion of shifts in people's views of one another, and by their fostering of a common cause. This cause is not about promoting one point of view, but about promoting the willingness to hear different points of view; it is not about winning or losing but about grappling with diverse human problems and seeing if there are ways to collectively address those problems. There have been tears and laughter in these groups, as well as tensions and expressions of tenderness. But in the end, for many at least, there is a distinct sense

---

[2] See: https://soundcloud.com/braverangelsmedia/conversations-introduction

that this is what our democratic republic should be about, and what our governmental relations should be about. This is what a *sane society* looks like.

That said, I also strongly feel, and have sensed from members of these groups, that something more is needed to deepen and extend the processes that they have set into motion. Some people, for example, have expressed the need to focus more concertedly on particular topics, or to expand their discussions with other members of the group or family, friends, neighbors, leaders in their communities. It is in this light, therefore, that I view the Experiential Democracy Dialogue as a useful complement to the Braver Angels' approach. Indeed, I view the Experiential Democracy Dialogue as a fruitful follow-up for those looking to intensify their interchange with others, delve more concertedly and more intimately into the differences that vex them, and potentially strengthen bonds that have lasting and expanding effects. Together, the Experiential Democracy Dialogue and Braver Angels (as well as similar forums), could inspire a potent brew, elevating and transforming our worlds.

Suggested Readings and Resources

Braver Angels (2020). Braver Angels website, Retrieved from www.braverangels.org

Bowles, N. (2019, November). How to get Trump voters and liberals to talk: Don't make anyone sit in a circle. *The New York Times.* Retrieved from https://www.nytimes.com/2019/11/03/us/trump-voters-liberals.html.

Ferguson, A., (2019, December). Can this marriage be saved? Applying the techniques of couples counseling to bring Reds and Blues back together again. *The Atlantic*, 86–90.

Fromm, E. (1955). *The sane society.* Holt, Rinehart, & Winston.

Graham, D. (2018, December). The bipartisan group that's not afraid of bipartisanship. *The Atlantic.* Retrieved from https://www.theatlantic.com/politics/archive/2018/12/better-angels-affective-polarization-political-divide/578539/.

Larson, C. (2020). *Experiential liberation within the socio-political divide: A phenomenological qualitative analysis of encounters with the liberal or conservative other.* [Manuscript in preparation]. Sponsored by the Fielding Institute, Santa Barbara, CA under a grant from the Kristine Mann Psychoanalytic Institute.

Conclusion:
We Have More in Common Than We Think

The above approaches illustrate the power of dialogue groups, and in particular concerted person-to-person contacts, in the facilitation of a more multifaceted, nuanced understanding of the "other." The more we can sit with the other both in ourselves and with actual others, the more we tend not only to appreciate moments that we never thought of before, but moments we never quite felt before either. This combination of fresh thinking and fresh feeling about otherness can in turn lead to creative realizations about the overlap among ostensibly "different" people. What conservative "Reds" and liberal "Blues" discover about each other's core values, for example, can lead to discussions or even action steps that converge toward a common purpose—like finding ways to protect the environment without abandoning workers or limiting crime without indulging in gun availability and so on.

While many may be skeptical, given the perceived state of our society, that enough people would be willing to enter into such dialogue processes, there is increasing evidence for them to reassess. A 2019 survey of 2100 Americans by a research group called "More in Common" found that—when it comes to political parties at least—Americans do not seem to be as polarized as they thought. In fact our perceptions of others (i.e., those on the liberal left and those on the conservative right) are often strikingly inaccurate, and there seems to be more opportunity for common ground than many people—on both "sides of the fence"—have believed for a very long time.

Here are the survey authors' findings, to which we all should pay close heed:

- Democrats and Republicans imagine that almost twice as many people on the other side hold extreme views than really do.
- On average, Democrats and Republicans believe that 55 percent of their opponents' views are extreme, but in reality only about 30 percent are.

- Americans with more partisan views hold more exaggerated views of their opponents.
- Members of America's "Exhausted Majority" have a narrower perception gap than either of the "Wings" (America's more politically partisan groups).
- Consumption of most forms of media—including talk radio, newspapers, social media, and local news—is associated with a wider perception gap.
- For example, people who consume news "most of the time" are almost three times as inaccurate as those who consume it "only now and then."
- Furthermore, those who post about politics on social media show a substantially larger perception gap than those who do not.
- Higher education among Democrats, but not Republicans, corresponds with a wider perception gap.
- For example, Democrats who hold a postgraduate degree are three times as inaccurate as those who did not graduate high school.
- This may be due in part to lower friendship diversity, as higher educated Democrats (but not Republicans) are more likely to say that "almost all" of their friends share their political views.
- The wider people's perception gap, the more likely they are to attribute negative personal qualities (like "hateful" or "brainwashed") to their opponents.
- Overall, Americans' views are more similar to their political opponents' views than they realize. Most Americans identify as either Democrats or Republicans, and while these sides often have very different approaches, as I have found in Braver Angels groups, they tend to share bedrock values such as the importance of personal and interpersonal safety, freedom, and fairness.

The authors conclude:

> While this research reveals disturbing trends, the overall message is positive: Americans often have more in common than they believe. Those with the greatest levels of hostility towards their political opponents typically understand them the least. This fundamental insight could be used as a basis for

a more productive *dialogue* between opposing camps and moving forward on critical threats and challenges confronting the United States as we enter the 2020s. [Note: the emphasis on "dialogue" is Kirk Schneider's]

What these findings—as well as Braver Angels' surveys—reveal is that there is more hope for the mending of social divides than it would at first appear, and that *dialogue*—personal and experiential meeting— are key to the process.   Without getting to know one another as persons, we are forever susceptible to the images and stereotypes that power brokers have a vested interest in shaping.

These findings also square with what we know about the process of psychotherapeutic healing. People's original fears or woundings are rarely on a par with what they perceive when confronted with those fears and woundings in a present and supportive context. This phenomenon is at the crux of what we call "exposure" therapies. As people learn to confront rather than to merely think about or dwell on a feared event, they gradually tend to see that event in a more nuanced and multifaceted light—a discovery-oriented light. This process also occurs in the consulting room when clients are able to face their therapists as the real and evolving people they are vs. the villains or adversaries they initially conceived them to be.

My hope is that this book will inspire more of us to engage in processes, such as interpersonal dialogues, that can help us undo the damage of our reactive judgments. The result, I believe, would be challenging, but it would also foster empathy, insight, and a collaborative spirit. My secondary hope is that such processes will help us change the structural oppression that drives so many of us into cultural, political, and consumerist silos; for the more we—deeply and broadly—learn about one another, the more we put ourselves in a position to be a society "of the people, by the people, and for the people."

Suggested Readings and Resources

Bellah, R., Madsen, R., Sullivan, M., Swidler, A., & Tipton, S. (1985). *Habits of the heart: Individualism and commitment in American life.* Perennial Library.

Carson, C. (2002). *A call to conscience: The landmark speeches of Dr. Martin Luther King Jr.* Grand Central Publishing.

Haidt, J. (2013). *The righteous mind: Why good people are divided by politics and religion.* Vintage.

Mindell, A. (2020). Worldwork IAPOP. Retrieved from http://worldwork.org/about/worldwork-deep-democracy/.

More in Common (2019). The perception gap. *More in Common.* Retrieved from https://perceptiongap.us/.

Rogers, C. (1986). The Rust Workshop: A personal overview. *Journal of Humanistic Psychology.* Retrieved from https://journals.sagepub.com/doi/10.1177/0022167886263003.

Rosenberg, M. (2015). *Nonviolent communications: A language of life.* Puddle Dancer Press.

Wills, G. (2006). *Lincoln at Gettysburg: The words that reshaped America.* Simon & Schuster.

Acknowledgments

This book owes its inspiration to many sources, including my colleagues who worked with me on the creation and development of the Experiential Democracy Dialogues. Among them are Shawn Rubin, Lisa Vallejos, Bob Kramer, Louis Hoffman, Theopia Jackson, David St. John, Jim Hernandez, Bob Edelstein, Nathaniel Granger, Rodger Broome, Candice Hershman, Ilene Serlin, Kenn Burrows, and my colleagues at the Existential–Humanistic Institute. I'm also appreciative of my colleagues in the Braver Angels Alliance groups and workshops, with special thanks to Ruth Littmann Ashkenazi for her perceptive feedback on earlier drafts of this book. I am also grateful for the leadership and creative inspiration of the co-founders of Braver Angels, William Doherty and David Blankenhorne, as well as to the many forerunners of the dialogue movement in America, from Martin Buber and Martin Luther King, to James Baldwin and William Buckley, and from Maurice Friedman to Carl Rogers and Libby and Len Traubman to Arnie Mindell and Marshall Rosenberg. Finally, I would like to express my deepest appreciation to all those courageous souls from philosophers and poets to religious and community leaders to indigenous sages and seers who prized the path of co-presence and co-existence. They are harbingers of our sustainment.

About the Author

Kirk J. Schneider, PhD, is a licensed psychologist and leading spokesperson for contemporary existential-humanistic psychology. Dr. Schneider is the current president of the Existential-Humanistic Institute (EHI), Council Member of the American Psychological Association (APA), past president of the Society for Humanistic Psychology (Division 32) of the APA, recent past editor of the *Journal of Humanistic Psychology*, a Member and Moderator for Braver Angels USA, and an adjunct faculty member at Saybrook University and Teachers College, Columbia University. Dr. Schneider has published over 200 articles, interviews, and chapters and has authored or edited 13 books including *The Spirituality of Awe, The Polarized Mind, Awakening to Awe, The Handbook of Humanistic Psychology, Existential-Humanistic therapy, Existential-Integrative Psychotherapy*, and *The Wiley World Handbook of Existential Therapy.* Dr. Schneider's work has been featured in *Scientific American,* the *New York Times, Psychology Today,* and many other health and psychology outlets. For more information on Dr. Schneider's work visit https://kirkjschneider.com.

Other Books by Kirk J. Schneider

The Polarized Mind: Why It's Killing Us and What to Do About It

What do a school shooter, a corporate swindler, and a bullheaded ideologue have in common? They all converge on what Dr. Kirk Schneider terms "the polarized mind." The polarized mind, which is the fixation on one point of view to the utter exclusion of competing points of view, is killing us—and has been for millennia. Drawing from the standpoint of existential psychology, this book details the basis for the polarized mind, how it has ravaged leaders and their cultures throughout history (up to and including our own time), and steps we urgently need to take to address the problem. Combining contemporary insights with centuries of cross-cultural, awe-inspired wisdom, Schneider offers solutions to this worldwide problem.

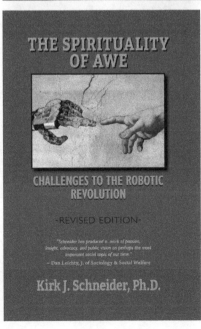

The Spirituality of Awe: Challenges to the Robotic Revolution (Revised Edition)

The robotic revolution is here and there's no going back. From the way we raise our children, to our work settings, to our governments, and even our wars, the quick fix-instant result society is roiling our world. Yet what is lost in this delirium is depth, the awesomeness, not just of our machines, but of our flesh, our capacity to feel, and our capacity to dwell in the miracle of the unknown. This book dwells in the miracle of the unknown. It is an intimate trek into the evolving spirituality of awe--the humility and wonder; sense of adventure toward life. Can we preserve awe--the arguable "heart" of humanity--in spite of and even in light of our technologies? Or will we devolve into mechanically driven puppets, numb to our possibilities, blind to our servitude? There is no more critical problem for our age."

CPSIA information can be obtained
at www.ICGtesting.com
Printed in the USA
LVHW010240140720
660628LV00016B/1485